FIVE PRACTICES OF FRUITFUL CONGREGATIONS

Robert Schnase
Bishop, Missouri Conference
The United Methodist Church

Abingdon Press
Nashville

Five Practices of Fruitful Congregations

Copyright © 2007 Robert Schnase

This book is printed on acid-free paper.

Library of Congress Cataloging-in-Publication Data

Schnase, Robert C., 1957-
Five practices of fruitful congregation / by Robert Schnase.
          p. cm.
ISBN-13: 978-0-687-64540-4
ISBN-10: 0-687-64540-9
1. Church renewal.   I. Title.
BV600.3.S353   2007
250—dc22   2006102088

Scripture quotations, unless otherwise indicated, are from the *New Revised Standard
Version of the Bible*, copyright © 1989, Division of Christian Education of the National
Council of the Churches of Christ in the United States of America.
Used by permission. All rights reserved.

11 12 13 14 15 16   −26 25 24 23 22

MANUFACTURED IN THE UNITED STATES OF AMERICA

CONTENTS

ACKNOWLEDGMENTS

Many people helped make this project possible. Bishop Bruce Ough first sparked my interest in a common language for congregational practices, and Bishop Janice Riggle Huie encouraged me to share these thoughts with a wider audience. My appreciation to both of them for their helpfulness, counsel, and support. My thanks to Dr. Lovett H. Weems, Jr., of the Lewis Center for Church Leadership and to Dr. Gil Rendle of the Alban Institute for reviewing the manuscript and offering suggestions. Judy Davidson's perceptive reading and gentle corrections have strengthened the work considerably. Brenda Stobbe provided many practical suggestions, and Erin Canine generously offered her creativity to help with the cover design.

My thanks also to the Missouri Conference Cabinet, the Seekers and Servants Sunday School Class at Community United Methodist Church in Columbia, and other pastors and laity who reviewed the work in progress and offered comments and encouragement. And my appreciation, of course, to my family, Esther, Karl, and Paul, for their patience with me as I turned to the task of writing on so many evenings in order to complete the book between other responsibilities.

Finally, I offer my special appreciation to the pastors, lay members, and congregations of the Missouri Conference of The United Methodist Church for the special privilege of serving with them in the awesome task of ministry given us by God. I give God thanks for all they do for the purposes of Christ and for The United Methodist Church. I pray our work together continues to be fruitful, joyful, and to the glory of God.

—Robert Schnase

INTRODUCTION

FIVE PRACTICES OF FRUITFUL CONGREGATIONS

Radical Hospitality. Passionate Worship. Intentional Faith Development. Risk-Taking Mission and Service. Extravagant Generosity. People are searching for a church shaped and sustained by these qualities. The presence and strength of these five practices demonstrate congregational health, vitality, and fruitfulness. By repeating and improving these practices, churches fulfill their mission to make disciples of Jesus Christ for the transformation of the world.

The words are contagious, and the congregations that use them behave differently. People know that the mission of the church is to make disciples of Jesus Christ, but they are seeking to understand how to fit this larger mission into their lives and into their churches in a practical way. These words capture the core process by which God uses congregations to make disciples—congregations offer the gracious invitation, welcome, and hospitality of Christ so that people experience a sense of belonging; God shapes souls and changes minds through worship, creating a desire to grow closer to Christ; God's Spirit nurtures people and matures faith through learning in community; with increased spiritual maturity, people discern God's call to help others through mission and service; and God inspires people to give generously of themselves so that others can receive the grace they have known. These fundamental practices are so critical to a congregation's mission that failure to perform them in an exemplary way results in congregational deterioration and decline. The words used to express these qualities are irresistible because they move us from abstract intentions to practical and personal directions for ministry. Once our mission becomes practical and personal, it becomes memorable and achievable.

These practices not only describe the congregational activities through which God works to draw people into relationship, they also chart the path for growth in personal discipleship. Followers of Christ aspire to grow in grace and in the knowledge and love of God. They do so by repeating, learning, and deepening their personal practice of gracious hospitality, by placing themselves regularly under the influence of God's Spirit in worship, by intentionally seeking to grow in Christ-likeness through learning in community, and by practicing compassion and generosity in concrete ways. In these simple practices of Christian discipleship, the prevenient, justifying, and sanctifying grace of God become visible, real, and life changing.

This book is designed to assist congregational leaders in holding a mirror to their own ministries in order to ask the questions, "How are we doing in practicing these qualities of ministry in our congregation? In our classes, choirs, small group ministries, mission teams, and leadership circles? How are we practicing these in our own personal discipleship? And how might we do better?" The task of repeating, deepening, extending, teaching, and improving these practices should fill church agendas, guide church boards, and shape leadership training.

The most visible way God knits people into community to fulfill the mission of Christ is through congregations, and these five practices give congregations a common language. As a result of working through a common language, faith communities become clear about their mission and confident about their future. Vibrant, fruitful, growing congregations are those that naturally practice these qualities and constantly seek ways to develop them further.

The language to express these characteristics has an interesting history. Bishop Bruce Ough searched Scripture for images to define congregational health for the Ohio West Conference of The United Methodist Church. Using the story of blind Bartimaeus, Bishop Ough identified four qualities—Radical Hospitality, Passionate Worship, Faith-Forming Relationships, and Risk-Taking Service. When I first heard these, I realized the extraordinary power of the simple, clear expressions. Some of Ough's words find their original source in other writings and in earlier attempts to articulate a common and bold language for the basic elements of community life in Christ. Upon reflection from my pastoral work, I added another quality that facilitates fruitful congregational ministry: Extravagant Generosity. With other minor revisions, I began to teach and preach among the United Methodist churches of the Missouri Conference, lifting up these five practices of congregational fruitfulness. Gradually, other church leaders introduced them as well, some adding revisions of their own.

The words have taken on a life of their own, and I have been amazed how these simple practices, intensified by strong adjectives, have captured the imagination of church leaders and have pushed them to a higher quality ministry. These practices have helped to create congregational strategies and have stimulated church councils, Sunday school classes, mission leaders, and pastors toward greater fruitfulness to the glory of God. Swept along by the Spirit of God, these words have leaped from conference to conference, congregation to congregation, and pastor to pastor as powerful tools provoking us to focused, intentional, and creative ministry.

These words are dangerous, edgy, and provocative. The practices are basic and fundamental to congregational strength, but the adjectives intensify them toward the unexpected and the exemplary. Vibrant, fruitful, growing congregations don't stop at practicing *friendly* hospitality, *helpful* service and mission, or *prudent* generosity. Their practices are extraordinary, exceptional, thorough, and extreme; they are *radical, passionate, intentional, risk-taking, and extravagant*. These words draw us in and cause us to ask provocative questions about our own congregational practices. No church that is vibrant, fruitful, and growing performs its ministry exactly as it did in the 1950s, and no pastor leading such a congregation is practicing ministry as she or he did in the 1970s or 1980s. Effective congregations change, improve, learn, and adapt to fulfill their mission, and these words push us to rethink our basic congregational culture, organization, and practice.

I have received these ideas and words from others, and now I commend them to a wider audience by writing this book, not to contain them or to own them but to give them greater life to the glory of God. People want the best for their churches. They long to fulfill the church's mission of making disciples, and they intuitively know that the congregation is the primary channel through which God forms people into the Body of Christ. And yet many laypersons and clergy have difficulty breaking down this universal mission into achievable tasks and practical strategies that strengthen churches. The purpose of this book is to give permission, focus, and encouragement for creative change and growth in ministry.

People of all ages hunger for congregations that embrace these qualities, churches that receive them graciously and invite them in, that connect them to God through authentic worship, that deepen their faith, and that stretch them so as to make a difference in the lives of others through service and generosity. Large or small; urban, suburban, or rural; churches with these qualities form disciples and transform communities.

Use this book in your Sunday school class or Bible study. Hold honest and positive conversations about your congregation's practices and how to move toward greater fruitfulness to the glory of God. Offer a five or six week study to focus on these essential disciplines of church life. Ask your church council members, mission leaders, and youth sponsors to enter into significant dialogue about how God uses congregations to make disciples of Jesus Christ through these practices. Let these practices give shape to retreat planning, priority setting, and strategy sessions for lay leaders, pastors, and staff.

Allow these practices to shape your own reflections about your church, your area of ministry, and your personal discipleship. Use them, amend them, deepen them, pray about them, and extend them so all may fulfill the greatest task ever entrusted to humankind, the work of sharing the good news we have seen and known in Jesus Christ.

CHAPTER ONE

THE PRACTICE OF RADICAL HOSPITALITY

*"Welcome one another, therefore, just as Christ has welcomed you,
for the glory of God." (Romans 15:7)*

1.

Vibrant, fruitful, growing congregations practice Radical Hospitality. Out of genuine love for Christ and for others, their laity and pastors take the initiative to invite, welcome, include, and support newcomers and help them grow in faith as they become part of the Body of Christ. Their members focus on those outside their congregation with as much passion as they attend to the nurture and growth of those who already belong to the family of faith, and they apply their utmost creativity, energy, and effectiveness to the task, exceeding all expectations.

The words *radical* and *hospitality* are not usually together in one phrase. To advance the church, perhaps they should be.

Christian hospitality refers to the active desire to invite, welcome, receive, and care for those who are strangers so that they find a spiritual home and discover for themselves the unending richness of life in Christ. It describes a genuine love for others who are not yet a part of the faith community, an outward focus, a reaching out to those not yet known, a love that motivates church members to openness and adaptability, a willingness to change behaviors in order to accommodate the needs and receive the talents of newcomers. Beyond intention, hospitality practices the gracious love of Christ, respects the dignity of others, and expresses *God's* invitation to others, not our own. Hospitality is a mark of Christian discipleship, a quality of Christian community, a concrete expression of commitment to grow in Christ-likeness by seeing ourselves as part of the community of faith, "not to be served but to serve" (Matthew 20:28). By practicing hospitality, we become part of God's invitation to new life, showing people that God in Christ values them and loves them.

Hospitality streams through Scripture. In Deuteronomy, God reminds the people of Israel to welcome the stranger, the sojourner, the wanderer. Why? "For you were strangers in the land of Egypt" (Deuteronomy 10:19).

We, too, were once strangers to the faith, residing outside the community where we now find rich resources of meaning, grace, hope, friendship, and service. We belong to the Body of Christ because of someone's hospitality. Someone invited us, encouraged us, received us, and helped us feel welcome—a parent, a spouse, a friend, a pastor, or even a stranger. By someone's love, we were engrafted onto the Body of Christ. If we had not felt welcomed and supported in some measure, we would not have stayed.

"A Ministry That Rocks!"

When Ann Mowery began her pastorate in a small, rural congregation in Missouri, attendance ran about 100 with a mix of ages, most of them older adults. After seven years, the attendance now regularly reaches 150 or more, and the congregation has built a new dining area and has renovated the youth room. The secret has been an active hospitality that has become contagious throughout the congregation. For instance, when a visiting mom felt self-conscious whenever her baby started to fuss during worship, Ann met with congregational leaders and they decided that they valued having young people so highly that they had to do something to ease the discomfort. To show support for the young mom, they bought a comfortable, well-padded rocking chair and placed it just behind the last pew of the small sanctuary. Word got around, and soon they had to have two more rocking chairs to accommodate the moms who found this congregation to be the friendliest around! Rocking chairs for moms, a cool-looking youth room for young people, a new extension that makes the building handicapped accessible—the pastor and the congregation use these to help communicate the priority they place on welcoming more and younger people.

Jesus says, "I was a stranger and you welcomed me" (Matthew 25:35). "Just as you did it to one of the least of these who are members of my family, you did it to me" (Matthew 25:40). We would change our behaviors toward strangers if we lived as if we really believed this!

A scenario at any church might look like this: a young single mom stands awkwardly in the foyer with her toddler, looking around at all the people she does not know on her first visit to a church. An acquaintance at work casually mentioned how she loved the music at her church and invited her to visit, but now she is not so sure this was a good idea. She is wondering about child care, self-conscious about the fussiness of her little one, unsure where the bathroom is, too timid to ask directions, doubting whether this is the right worship service for her, or whether this is even the right church. Where is she to sit, what is it going to feel like to sit alone with her child, and what if her little one makes too much noise? She feels the need for prayer; for some connection to others; and for something to lift her above the daily grind of her job, the unending bills, the conflicts with her ex-husband, and her worries for her child.

Now, imagine what would happen if people took Jesus' words seriously. They would look at this woman and the whole bundle of hopes and anxieties, desires and discomforts that she carries and think, "This is a member of Jesus' family, and Jesus wants us to treat her as we would treat Jesus himself if he were here." With this in mind, what would be the quality of the welcome, the efforts to ease the awkwardness? What would be the enthusiasm to help, to serve, to graciously receive and support and encourage? Taking Jesus seriously changes congregational behavior.

At every turn, the disciples seem ready to draw boundaries and distinctions that keep people at a distance from Jesus. They have a thousand reasons to ignore, avoid, and sometimes thwart the approach of people, reminding Jesus that some of these people are too young, too sick, too sinful, too old, too Roman, too blind, or too Gentile to deserve his attention. Jesus teaches, "Whoever welcomes one such child in my name welcomes me" (Matthew 18:5). In every instance, Jesus radically challenges the disciples' expectations by overstepping the boundaries to invite people in. Hospitality has us seeing people as Jesus sees them and seeing Jesus in the people God brings before us.

But Jesus' hospitality extends beyond the cordial welcome we offer when someone appears at the threshold of the church and then feel good that we've completed our obligations. Jesus tells a parable about himself, saying, "Then [the king] said to his slaves . . . 'Go therefore into the main streets, and invite everyone you find to the wedding banquet'" (Matthew 22:8-9). Following Jesus' example of gathering people into the Body of Christ, inviting them to the banquet of God's gracious love requires intentional focus on those outside the community of faith. Jesus' example of hospitality demands an unceasingly invitational posture that we carry with us into our world of work and leisure and into our practice of neighborliness and community service. It involves seeing ourselves as sent out by Christ and going out of our way, even at the risk of a sense of awkwardness and inconvenience, to invite people into some aspect of the church's ministry. Hospitality is prayer, work, habit, practice, and initiative for the purposes of Christ.

Paul implores the followers of Christ to practice an active hospitality. "Welcome one another, therefore, just as Christ has welcomed you, for the glory of God" (Romans 15:7). The grace received in Christ places upon Christians the joyful gift and challenging task of offering others the same welcome they themselves have received. The letter of Hebrews cautions, "Do not neglect to show hospitality to strangers, for by doing that some have entertained angels without knowing it" (Hebrews 13:2). The people welcomed into a congregation may prove to be those individuals through whom God graces others' lives. As the community of faith receives and assimilates newcomers and accepts their spiritual gifts and natural talents, their life experiences and faith perspectives, the church changes and ministry expands. God uses newcomers to breathe new life into congregations.

John Wesley and the early Methodists practiced hospitality in ways so radical in their day that many traditional church leaders found their activities offensive. Wesley preached to thousands on roadsides and in open fields in order to reach coal miners, field laborers, factory workers, the underclass, and the poorest of the poor. He invited them into community and nurtured in them a strong sense of belonging as he organized societies and classes for mutual accountability, support, and care. Wesley taught of God's prevenient grace: the preceding, preparing grace that draws people to God.

According to Wesley, before people ever consciously come to faith, they have inner desires for relationship to God that are stifled, forgotten, neglected, ignored, or denied. By the grace that precedes awareness or decision, God creates readiness for faith in the individual and fosters the nascent eagerness to please God. By God's grace, people may be more ready than we realize to accept the invitation and initiative of Christ that comes through gracious hospitality. Just as God's prevenient grace enables people to choose to move closer to God, so also God's grace works through the church to offer an initiating, surrounding, inviting love. Through the practice of Radical Hospitality, the early Methodists as well as United Methodists today express the gracious welcome of God in Christ. God seeks relationship to people. God's grace activates interest and eagerness for relationship just as God's grace shapes the invitational posture of congregations to reach out in love.

2.

I served one congregation that wanted to deepen its understanding of hospitality, growing beyond the practical steps recommended by books on evangelism, assimilation, and visitor follow-up. We had the techniques right—helpful signage, accessible parking, trained greeters, and a system of visitor follow-up. But we sought a culture of hospitality that extended into our Sunday school classes, mission teams, choirs, and youth ministry. I invited ten church leaders to commit with me to a series of lunches for in-depth study and reflection on welcoming people into the Body of Christ. These people loved the church, lived the faith, and were those whom others naturally followed. They arranged their work schedules and family responsibilities to attend for an hour and a half, once a week, for six weeks. I provided copies of a small book entitled *Widening the Welcome of Your Church,* (Fred Bernhard and Steve Clapp, Lifequest Publishing, 1996) and sent out a letter listing the short chapters that we would read each week and the Scriptures that would guide our conversation. Speaking about our faith journeys was the key to our time together, not the content of the book.

In our first session, we shared how each of us had come to be a part of the Body of Christ. We discussed questions such as, "Who had invited us or brought us to church? Where did we become involved, and what type of service or activity did we first attend? How did we feel about those earliest encounters with the Body of Christ? What made us feel welcome? What difficulties did we have to overcome?" We talked about people, places, services, ministries, pastors, and studies that God used to form us. Some remembered making attempts to enter into churches from which they felt resistance, obstacles, coldness. Next, we talked about what had brought each one to First Church, the congregation to which we belonged at that time. How had we first heard about the church? What was our first worship experience like with this congregation? What strengthened us and made us feel welcome, or what made it hard to connect? Many were surprised to hear how difficult it had been for some to feel warmly received or how long it had taken. Others lifted up particular people or events that had opened the door for them and helped them feel they belonged to the community of faith. It was an honest and profoundly moving conversation, intermingling the experiences of those who were long-term members with those who had joined recently.

During another session, we discussed the theological meaning of the church as the Body of Christ and delved into the "why" of invitation, welcome, and hospitality. Why do we invite and welcome people into our midst? So that our statistics look better to impress the Bishop? In order to survive as an institution or to develop a stronger financial base? We discussed the fundamental purpose for which the church exists—to draw people into relationship with God through Jesus Christ—and how this changes lives. To live in community with others is part of God's plan and intention for us. A congregation is a school for love, the place where God's Spirit forms us and the place where we learn how to give love to and receive love from friends, neighbors, and strangers. The church is the presence of Christ in the world, the means by which God knits us into community in order to transform our lives and the lives of those around us. To keep the discussion fruitful, we avoided the premature focus on techniques and strategies, and concentrated

> **"Fresh Flowers, Free Lunches, No Offering"**
>
> As a Bishop, I enjoy the privilege of seeing many diverse settings for ministry. While looking for signs of Radical Hospitality in a fast-growing suburban congregation, I was struck by a dozen little extra-effort details that helped them attract high-paced suburban families. There were clearly marked parking places for visitors, amiable and helpful greeters, professionally designed brochures about a variety of ministries, an information station, special electronics for the hearing impaired, a well-supplied "cry room" for babies, and pagers for parents with children in the nursery. There were also fresh-cut flowers in the immaculate bathrooms, attractive bins outside the front doors so that kids could drop off their fast-food trash on their way in the door, and several seats with arms in the worship center for seniors who need the extra push when standing up.
>
> An open country church in a sparse rural county decided to honor and show appreciation for a special group of people one day each month. The first month, they made sack lunches, added a personal note of thanks, and delivered them to all the

on the fundamental purpose of Christian hospitality.

In one session, we talked honestly about the greatest gifts we had received through the church from our relationship with Christ. People described how First Church had helped them rear their children, and they recounted tender moments of grace that had sustained them during seasons of grief. They gave God thanks for close friendships formed in the church that had shaped their lives and given them insight for dealing with life's challenges. Moreover, we considered honestly, without boasting or any negative spirit of pride, what had been the greatest contribution each of us had ever made to building the Body of Christ. Some talked about teaching junior high Sunday school students, others about mission projects they had led, and others

farmers in the fields for several miles around. Next, they served volunteer fire fighters, then school teachers, and then county workers. Over the year, more than a hundred people received these unexpected reminders of the hospitality of the church.

An urban African-American congregation announces before receiving the offering that visitors shouldn't feel like they have to give anything. "You're our guests, and we want you simply to receive the blessings of this worship. We're glad you are here."

In all three churches, the pastor and congregation are focused on welcoming those from outside and inviting them inside. And at all three churches, the pastors give a positive no-pressure invitation during the closing hymns of every worship service. "If anyone would like to enter into the membership of the church by transfer from another church or by profession of faith, you are invited to come forward. We'd love to welcome you into the ministry of our congregation. Or if you would like to talk about this with the pastor, please talk to me after the service or call me during the week, and I'd be happy to visit with you."

about financial gifts they had given for special projects. After all had shared their experiences, I suggested that we think about another contribution that we may have made or should seek to make. The greatest contribution we can make to the Body of Christ is inviting someone else or helping a newcomer feel genuinely welcome so that she or he receives what we have received.

Sometimes members forget that churches offer something people need. What do people need that congregations offer? In *Leading Beyond the Walls* (Abingdon Press, 2002), Adam Hamilton reminds us (on p. 21) that every church should be clear about the answers to the questions, "Why do people need Christ? Why do people need the church? And why do people need this particular congregation?" Is it too presumptuous, self-righteous, or arrogant to perceive a responsibility, or even a calling, to invite and encourage others so that they may receive what we have received?

What do those of us who belong to a community of faith receive that our neighbors need? Theologically, the answer may be "a relationship to God through Jesus Christ." This is too abstract for most, and for many it feels heavy-laden with negative experiences of intrusive and aggressive evangelistic styles. But the question persists. How do we express with integrity and clarity what we hope others receive? What do people need from the church?

People need to know God loves them, that they are of supreme value, and that their life has significance. People need to know that they are not alone; that when they face life's difficulties, they are surrounded by a community of grace; and that they do not have to figure out entirely for themselves how to cope with family tensions, self-doubts, periods of despair, economic reversal, and the temptations that hurt themselves or others. People need to know the peace that runs deeper than an absence of conflict, the hope that sustains them even through the most painful periods of grief, the sense of belonging that blesses them and stretches them and lifts them out of their own preoccupations. People need to learn how to offer and accept forgiveness and how to serve and be served. As a school for love, the church becomes a congregation where people learn from one another how to love. People need to know that life is not having something to live on but something to live for, that life comes not from taking for oneself but by giving of oneself. People need a sustaining sense of purpose.

Having said that, the last thing people want is to be told by someone else what they need! Inviting people into Christ does not involve pounding people with "oughts" and "shoulds." Some people recognize their needs, and they search for meaning, for others, and for God. But most people discover their need for God's grace and for the love of Christ through the experience of receiving it. There are countless stories of people who did not know how hungry they were for genuine community until they experienced it, of people who never knew they needed the connection to God which worship fosters until they regularly attended, and of people who sensed something missing from their lives and didn't know what it was until they immersed themselves in regular service to others in need. When we invite people into a Bible study, to a Christian support group for single moms, to a prayer ministry, to sing with the praise team, to help with a service project, or to serve at a food bank for the poor, we are providing an avenue by which the Spirit of God shapes the human soul. By such ministries, the Spirit fills the empty spaces in people's lives, and God's inviting grace calls them out of themselves and into the world of Christ's service.

The power of an invitation to change a person's life must never be under-estimated! Perhaps that is how God changed each one of us.

When I worked in a clergy-training program at a hospital, I was called to the emergency room to support an older man whose wife had been brought to the hospital by ambulance. They had started their morning with no idea how events would unfold that day. After shopping, they stopped at a restaurant, and while she was eating, she suffered a heart attack and was rushed to the hospital. Shortly after I arrived in the small consultation room with the husband, a doctor approached him to announce that his wife had died. The doctor handed me an envelope that contained her wedding ring, her necklace, and her eyeglasses to give to him. Needless to say, the man was stunned with grief. After a few minutes together, I offered to call his pastor. He did not have a pastor because they attended no church. I asked if I could call a family member to come take him home, and he told me his family was scattered across the country, living many hundreds of miles away. I asked if I could call a co-worker to be with him, and he told me he had retired years before from work in another city. What about a neighbor I could call? He told me that he and his wife didn't know the names of the other residents in the apartment since they'd only lived there three years. I helped him with the paper work, offered a prayer as I held his hands in mine, handed him the envelope that contained the jewelry and glasses, escorted him to the exit, and watched him walk away alone to cope with the shocking news of the day and to grasp its meaning for himself all on his own.

Life is not meant to be that way. God intends for people to live their lives interlaced by the grace of God with others, to know the gift and task of community from birth to death, to have the interpretive structures of faith to sustain them through times of joy and periods of desperate agony, to have the perspective of eternity, and to "take hold of the life that really is life" (1 Timothy 6:19).

In most communities, 40 to 60 percent of people have no church relationship. A majority of our neighbors on the streets where we live do not know the name of a pastor to call when they face an unexpected grief. Most of our co-workers have a few close friends and a circle of acquaintances but do not know the sustaining grace that a church offers. Most of the families with whom we travel to our children's soccer tournaments and band concerts, most of the fine students we meet from the university, and most of the people who repair our cars and serve us in restaurants do not have a forum where they learn about the essentials of peace, justice, genuine repentance, forgiveness, love, and unmerited grace. Most of those who crowd the malls where we shop, attend the ballgames we enjoy, and sit behind us at movies and concerts do not know what it's like to join their voices with others in song and how this lifts the spirit in ways beyond words. Most of those who share our benches at bus stops, who sit across from us in waiting rooms, who take their children to the school down the block from us do not have a community that prompts them to service, to take risks for others, and to practice generosity.

Practicing hospitality is not launching a membership drive for a civic organization or inviting people to join a club in order to enhance revenue through dues. We invite people into that mysteriously sustaining community that finds its purpose in the life, death, and resurrection of Jesus Christ. In the life he lived—the lessons he taught, the people he touched, the healing he offered, the forgiveness he gave, the love he showed, and the sacrifice he made—is the life that really is life.

"We're such a friendly church. We do fine with hospitality." Sometimes the greatest strength of churches and classes and choirs is also their greatest weakness. Church members love each other so much that their lives are so intertwined and their interests so interwoven that church groups become impenetrable to new people. Closeness closes out new people who feel like outsiders looking in, and those on the inside don't even notice. Church members feel content because their own needs are met.

Hospitality means we pray, plan, prepare, and work toward the purpose of helping others receive what we have received in Christ. Hospitality is more than common politeness to newcomers, name tags for greeters, or a few visitor parking spaces, although these are important. Hospitality is a quality of spiritual initiative, the practice of an active and genuine love, a graciousness unaffected by self-interest, an opening of ourselves and our faith community to receive others. When the spirit of Christ's hospitality pervades a congregation, then every choir, youth ministry, adult Sunday school class, mission team, Bible study, and outreach ministry regularly asks itself, "How are we doing at inviting others and supporting newcomers into our part of the church family? And how can we improve?"

3.

If the biblical quality of hospitality includes all these things, why intensify it with the word *radical*? What is Radical Hospitality?

Radical means "arising from the source" and describes practices that are rooted in the life of Christ and that radiate into the lives of others. *Radical* means "drastically different from ordinary practice, outside the normal," and so it provokes practices that exceed expectations, that go the second mile, that take welcoming the stranger to the max. By *radical*, I don't mean wild-eyed, out of control, or in your face. I mean people offering the absolute utmost of themselves, their creativity, their abilities, and their energy to offer the gracious invitation and reception of Christ to others. Churches characterized by Radical Hospitality are not just friendly and courteous, passively receiving visitors warmly. Instead, they exhibit a restlessness because they realize so many people do not have a relationship to a faith community. They sense a calling and responsibility to pray, plan, and work to invite others and to help them feel welcome and to support them in their faith journeys. They desire to learn about inviting and welcoming more people and younger people and more diverse people into their congregation.

Churches practicing Radical Hospitality offer a surprising and unexpected quality of depth and authenticity in their caring for the stranger. Newcomers intuitively sense that. "These people really care about me here. They really want the best for me. I'm not just a number, a customer, or an outsider here. I'm being invited with them into the Body of Christ." This is Radical Hospitality. Congregations surprise newcomers with a glimpse of the unmerited gracious love of God that they see in Christ.

Radical Hospitality shapes the work of every volunteer and staff member. All pray, plan, and work so that their specific ministries with children, missions, the facility, worship, music, and study are done with excellence and with special attention to inviting others in and helping them feel welcome. The word *radical* intensifies expectations and magnifies the central importance of this invitational element of our life together in Christ. Radical Hospitality goes to the extremes, and we do it joyfully, not superficially, because we know our invitation is the invitation of Christ.

Churches marked by this quality work hard to figure out how best to anticipate others' needs and to make them feel at home in their ministries. All churches offer some form of hospitality, but Radical Hospitality describes churches that strive without ceasing to exceed expectations to accommodate and include others.

A congregation marked by such hospitality adopts an invitational posture that changes everything it does. Members work with a heightened awareness of the person who is not present, the neighbors, friends, and co-workers who have no church home. With every ministry, they consider how to reach those who are not yet present.

Aspiring to Radical Hospitality changes the church completely. Two examples illustrate this change: Vacation Bible School and the Board of Trustees.

Most churches, large and small, offer some form of Vacation Bible School for children during the summer. If we asked some churches, "What's the purpose of Vacation Bible School?" we might receive the answer, "So that our children can have a fun experience while school is out." What kind of purpose is that? If the purpose of Vacation Bible School is simply for children to have fun, then why not load them into the church van, take them to the mall, and let them spend time with all their friends? Such a purpose cannot sustain a children's ministry with integrity.

Other churches answer, "The purpose of Vacation Bible School is so that our children and grandchildren can hear about God and learn the stories of the faith through songs, crafts, drama, and other fun ways of teaching." VBS now serves a higher purpose. Clearly stating this purpose guides the leaders in selecting volunteers; choosing curriculum; planning communications; and scheduling dates, times, and locations. If someone brings a friend, or if children from a new family in the neighborhood show up, leaders view it as an added delight, a good opportunity to warmly welcome them. This attitude is basic Christian hospitality.

Now imagine a church that takes this one step further and claims, "The purpose of Vacation Bible School is so that our children and grandchildren and the children of the neighborhood can hear about God and learn the stories of the faith so that more families become actively involved in the life of the church." Radical Hospitality makes an obvious difference. To focus VBS not just on the members' own children but also upon those outside the church, guides planners to use other forms of communications about the event—the town newspaper, posters in local businesses, announcements on the radio, flyers on bulletin boards in laundromats. To be driven by this purpose means that the church might change the location, dates, and times. For instance, if the church wanted to use the talents of working moms or dads, this might change the traditional meeting times. This purpose means that the planners recruit leadership differently, particularly choosing teachers and musicians who have a gift for making newcomers feel at home, perhaps even inviting some of the current visitors and newest members to teach and to help. Enlivened by this new purpose, leaders might collaborate with other churches, invite musicians who relate best to young people, and hold some of the programs in a school, park, or neighborhood apart from the church. Such an invitational posture inspires planners to gather information on each child who attends so that the pastors can follow up with families through notes of appreciation, invitations to other ministries, and a phone call to invite them to worship. Planners would evaluate their success not just by how many of their own children participate, but by how many new families the church touches and how many eventually move to greater involvement.

Applying Radical Hospitality changes the way churches plan for children's ministries. Volunteer and material resources are aligned toward the objective of inviting and welcoming people in the name of Christ. With the Spirit's prompting, there is no end to how far a congregation might go with this. Some churches offer Sidewalk Sunday School, sending vans full of teachers into neighborhoods full of kids in areas beyond the usual range of the church's outreach, where they set up for an hour of stories, singing, crafts, and teaching close to where the children live and play. That's Radical Hospitality, God's Spirit moving the church family to take initiatives it would never risk on its own.

Radical Hospitality means that the church is not just another social club but the Body of Christ constantly seeking to fulfill the mission of Christ. There's no self-satisfied attitude, "Now that my needs are met, I'm happy." People offer themselves to Christ by offering Christ to others.

Imagine Radical Hospitality shaping all ministries—Sunday Schools, choirs, mission projects, youth work, worship life, and pastoral care—in the same way it changes the purposes and practices for Vacation

---

"Multiple Blessings"

A large, growing church celebrated the birth of triplets to a couple in the congregation. LeeAnn, the church secretary, believed that the extraordinarily overwhelming task of parenting triplets deserved the prayerful support of the congregation. How could the church best minister to parents of multiple births? She contacted the parents of twins she knew in the congregation and asked for their insight. Soon, the church staff became aware of two other sets of twins, born to families connected to the church's day school. A few weeks later, the church launched a new ministry—a support group for parents of multiple births, called Twins and More! The church provided high quality childcare, invited a family counselor to lead the first gathering, announced the ministry in the local newspaper, and then let the parents establish their own agenda for discussions and activities. Soon several families—members, visitors, and some unrelated to the church—began to attend and then get involved with the church. Radical Hospitality involves seeing a need and taking the initiative to reach out to help!

Bible School. If each ministry simply changes one element of its task to reflect the Radical Hospitality of Christ, there's no end to what God could accomplish.

Let's look at another example. Most Boards of Trustees are comprised of long-time members who have general experience in business, law, finances, or property management. They see that church property is properly insured, the air-conditioning works, and the roof doesn't leak. In many churches, their job is simply to deal with the crises and complaints that arise about the facilities, and they focus primarily on property, not people. They practice basic hospitality, seeing that people are safe and moderately comfortable while attending services and ministries.

Now imagine a Board of Trustees that practices Radical Hospitality, viewing their work as a ministry that ensures the facilities communicate maximum hospitality, an unmistakable sense of welcome, and complete accessibility. The Board members might say, "Our purpose is to ensure that these facilities serve the highest purposes of ministry in Christ's name, and we dedicate ourselves to the highest standards of excellence as we make the facilities as useful, inviting, friendly, and open as we possibly can."

Such a Board deals responsibly with insurance and maintenance, but it doesn't stop there. It constantly searches for new ways to make the church look fresh, appealing, inviting, easy to navigate, safe, clean, and attractive. Board members are unsettled with anything less than the best, and they take immediate action when they see messy restrooms, peeling paint, musky carpets, inadequate lighting, potholes in parking lots, distracting and inadequate sound systems in worship, or playgrounds overgrown with weeds. Church members don't allow their houses to fall into disrepair, and they never send their own grandchildren into an unkempt backyard full of unsafe play equipment. Why do they let God's house fall into such disrepair? Facilities speak a message to people about what church members think of themselves, how importantly they take their mission, how confidently they see the future of their church. Our buildings tell the world what our church thinks about children, senior citizens, persons with disabilities, and visitors. What message are we sending? Radical Hospitality isn't just for the program committees of the church. Trustees have a ministry to fulfill as well.

Facilities work against the witness of welcome when newcomers struggle to figure out confusing and outdated signs, convoluted hallways, and staircases that insiders have grown accustomed to but which overwhelm visitors. Where are the Trustees? Radical Hospitality pushes them beyond discussing merely insurance and leaky roofs.

It is easier to create a culture of hospitality in a building that itself communicates welcome and speaks of optimism about the future.

Most young adults work in newer buildings with modern lighting, contemporary colors and textures, and fire security systems that make them feel safe. They eat at restaurants and sleep in hotels and attend movies that meet high standards. They are accustomed to quality and cleanliness in restrooms, and they come with high expectations about the safety of the nursery and classrooms for their children. Many feel like they're traveling back in time when they visit a church and see the 1950s institutional green paint, the rust-stained floors and cramped toilets in restrooms, the dim lights in hallways, and the absence of smoke detectors and handicapped accessibility. We can do better.

I visited a church that had changed the time of its worship services more than two years before and had moved the pastor's office to the former high school Sunday school room. Two years after these changes, the sign in front still had the old worship schedule, and the one on the pastor's office still described it as the youth room. The incident sounds quaint, and church members found the delay in updating signs amusing, like a family joke that several recounted with self-deprecating good humor. But they might as well have hung a sign that said, "For Insiders Only," on the front of the church, and one that said, "You're on your own. Good luck!" in the hallway. Nothing about the facility said, "Welcome. We want you to feel at home here." We can do better.

All churches say they warmly welcome people who use wheelchairs or walkers. Our buildings speak a different message: "Sure we welcome people with disabilities here…as long as they can climb up the stairs and slide into the pews just like everyone else!" We can do better.

4.

Radical Hospitality stretches us, challenges us, and pulls out of us our utmost creativity and hard work to offer the welcome of Christ.

Churches that practice Radical Hospitality don't merely have ushers and greeters; they also train them, teach them, prepare them, and make their service a vital ministry. Their ushers and greeters don't merely point, they escort; they don't merely pass out papers, they make people feel at ease.

They take note of names and introduce visitors to the pastor and to others. They constantly seek to understand the perspective of the newcomer and to see church practices and facilities from the visitor's point of view so they can anticipate those needs.

Churches that practice Radical Hospitality don't merely have a hospitality committee, they make Christian invitation and welcome a vital part of the culture of the church, an expectation of every member and of every Sunday School class, Bible study, choir, and mission team. Every ministry invests serious time to plan, pray for, invite, and receive newcomers, and to teach current members how to be more welcoming.

Churches characterized by Radical Hospitality do not just communicate with their own members about programs and ministries; they intentionally, strategically, and frequently communicate to the public through mailings, brochures, posters, banners, newspapers, websites, and signs. All of their communication is "visitor friendly," free of insider jargon and acronyms. They extend hospitality through advertising, signs, and the media by revealing publicly what the church represents, communicating that it is open to all and that all are invited and welcomed.

Churches that practice Radical Hospitality don't coast after Christmas and Easter. They carefully follow up with letters or phone calls to visitors who attend well-publicized Christmas Eve and Easter Sunday services, and they plan programs on compelling topics a couple of weeks after major services so that they have an appealing ministry to which they can invite their Easter and Christmas visitors. They never miss an opportunity to woo people into the life of the church.

Churches that practice Radical Hospitality constantly learn from other churches how to do better with hospitality, visitor follow-up, and newcomer assimilation. Pastors and laity read the literature about how to become more inviting, and they discuss it and put plans into action. They evaluate their work honestly and solicit feedback from newcomers about what helps in offering the genuine welcome of Christ.

Churches that practice Radical Hospitality do not reduce lists, remove names, ignore inactive members, save postage, and take the easiest way. They focus on how to communicate better with greater numbers of people, and they constantly develop lists of visitors, active and inactive members, Christmas and Easter attendees, constituents, day school parents, scout families, and infrequent guests in order to invite them to special services, new ministries, or service projects. They don't give up on anyone.

Churches that practice Radical Hospitality do not merely expect current classes and choirs and ministries to invite and welcome people; they also launch new ministries and classes especially aimed at including those who are new. They're not afraid of failure and know that even if only a handful of people gather in Christ's name, a great harvest is promised.

Churches that practice Radical Hospitality do not look only at the numbers, corralling people through perfunctory processes to get them to join. Instead, they genuinely engage people, listen to them, and help them feel accepted, respected, connected, needed, involved, and loved. They focus on the ultimate goal of helping newcomers grow into the Body of Christ's people.

Edwards Deming, the genius of organizational systems, observed that "a system produces what it is designed to produce." In this intentionally redundant statement, he reminds us that a system is aligned to get the results it is getting, and it will not get any other kind of results unless something changes.

How is your church going? Is worship attendance increasing or decreasing? Is membership trending older each year or getting younger with the addition of new members? Is the number of classes, studies, services, and missions increasing or decreasing? If yours is like most congregations in mainline denominations, it is declining in numbers, increasing in expenses, and aging in membership at an accelerating rate with each passing year. From Deming, church leaders realize that if they set up a task force and asked its members to work late into the night to develop a congregational plan that would cause attendance to fall by 5 percent each year and the median age to increase each year, they would come back with a plan that looks exactly like what their church is doing now! Congregational systems are perfectly aligned to get the results they are getting, and that means uninterrupted decline for most churches.

Something must change. People getting mad and leaving is not the cause of our decline. Members simply grow old and die, and no one takes their places. The church has a "front door" problem rather than a "back door" problem. People are not entering into the life of the church at a rate that matches or exceeds the number maturing and dying. In many cases, we have not passed along the faith to our own children and grandchildren.

To become a vibrant, fruitful, growing congregation requires a change of attitudes, practices, and values. Good intentions are not enough. Too many churches want more young people as long as they act like old people, more newcomers as long as they act like old-timers, more children as long as they are as quiet as adults, more ethnic families as long as they act like the majority in the congregation.

We can do better. It takes practicing Radical Hospitality, and all the redirecting of energy and resources and volunteer time that comes with this. Church leaders can't keep doing things the way they have always done them.

Little changes have big effects, and change can happen in a hurry. I've known people who have joined a church and remained lifelong members because of the personal handwritten letter they received following the first week they visited from a member they did not know. People have joined the church because when they first visited and their baby fussed, a woman leaned forward and said, "Don't worry. That's the way I feel about this sermon, too. But come back, they get better!" Then the woman offered to walk the baby in the foyer so the visitors could attend to the sermon. People have joined for a lifetime of faithfulness and service because they remember when they had their children in the weekday preschool and were not attending services, the pastor nevertheless visited them in the hospital when one of their parents was dying. Attending to the smallest of details and practices changes the culture of the church.

I've seen small churches that painted their nurseries, trained their nursery staff, replaced the playground equipment, and within weeks word-of-mouth carried the message of their special care for children to others, and attendance grew from forty-five members to fifty-five. And it all started with a simple paint job!

Imagine if every committee, choir, class, and service and staff member of a congregation agreed to prayerfully consider changing one practice this year to accommodate younger adults. The trustees might put diaper changing tables in the restrooms, the choir might prepare a musical that includes children, an adult class might gather funds for nursery services for a Bible study, the men's group might host a father-son event, and the pastor might invite all the young adult members and visitors to a get-acquainted dinner. If every ministry changed a little toward welcoming younger people, the cumulative effect might change the direction of the church.

I've seen large congregations try audacious new tactics for welcoming newcomers, with no assurance of success. From safe and easily supportable new initiatives, such as Parents' Night Out programs for young families or Brown Bag Bible Studies in workplace cafeterias, to more edgy ministries, such as alternative services in strip center malls for the "tattoos and piercings" crowd, these churches have let the Radical Hospitality they see in Christ lead them in creative directions.

The willingness to risk something new creates a buzz and a stir in the community that strengthens participation in all other ministries of the church. In ways no one understands, when the contemporary services begin to welcome new people in a manner that exceeds expectations, often the traditional Sunday school class for older members grows as well. Word-of-mouth is still the most important form of human communication, and when people talk about congregations as places that make people feel welcome and loved, then the church thrives.

How are we doing with our hospitality? How can we make it the Radical Hospitality we see in the life, teachings, death, and resurrection of Christ? How are we doing as a church, as a Sunday school class, in our worship services and mission projects and youth programs? How can we do better?

5.

A church changes its culture one person at a time. Radical Hospitality begins with a single heart, a growing openness, a prayerful desire for the highest good of a stranger. It begins when one person treats another respectfully and loves the stranger enough to overcome the internal hesitations to invite that person into the life of Christ's church.

Personal responsibility for the task of Christian discipleship is avoided by redirecting the conversation to programs and strategies and new initiatives. Members easily point toward the pastor, the staff, or a particular committee and say, "If they would only . . ." Or, "What they should do is . . ." Members blame and scapegoat and find fault for why things don't work better, and they deny and ignore and avoid their own complicity in the stagnation of their churches. In a Sunday school class or worship service, responsibility for welcoming the newcomer is diffused, and everyone assumes someone else is doing what needs to be done. That's why so many visitors feel alone and shunned, even in a crowd of friendly people. This won't change until each person takes responsibility for practicing Radical Hospitality as obedience to the ministry of Christ. Church members have to mature from "they ought" to "I will."

An invitation is not complicated. In the first chapter of John's gospel, Jesus' invitation was simple: "Come and see" (John 1:39). His disciples then used the same language to invite others. People don't need to know the answers to all the questions of faith and life to invite someone to church. They don't need to exaggerate or persuade or say more than is true. They simply and naturally find their own way of saying to acquaintances and those with whom they share common activities, "Come and see."

The lay people I've seen do this best do not fill their invitations with "oughts and shoulds." They don't make people feel guilty or nag them incessantly. They pray constantly for the wisdom of right timing, and when it feels natural, they tell about a service project they are working on at the church or a music team that's doing a special this weekend, and they say, "We'd love to have you join us if you have nothing else going on." On Monday mornings when co-workers talk about their weekend activities, they're not afraid to say, "I so enjoyed the youth musical last night at my church… I wish you could have heard them," or "I just loved working on the Habitat for Humanity project with my church, but my back is killing me today. And yet it means more than I can say to be able to work on a project like that." They find their own voice and say in their own way, "Come and see."

Or when someone new starts work at the office or someone moves into the neighborhood, in addition to the standard gestures of welcome and support, without feeling self-conscious they say, "And if you're looking for a church, I'd be happy to tell you about mine. I love it, and it's meant the world to my family, and we'd love to have you come with us sometime." At other times, when they know someone faces a difficulty in their marriage or suffers the grief of loss, they're not afraid to say, "Something that helped me was talking to my pastor. I know she'd be willing to talk to you, too. If you want her name or would like for me to call her, I'd be happy to help and I know she would, too."

Do these simple invitations feel natural? Are they something people feel comfortable doing? People have no reluctance telling others where they get their hair cut, where they get their car fixed, where they like to eat. And yet, concerning the most important relationship Christian disciples have—the one to God through Christ's church—they feel hesitant to speak. They don't want to intrude or appear pushy or sound too fanatically religious. But think of all the church means, all that relationship to God means, the perspective of faith, the understandings of life, the relationships gained, the sense of meaning and connection and contribution experienced. Why wouldn't we desire these things for the people we respect and love, and for the neighbors and co-workers we share our lives with? We pray to God for those who are in our lives. Why not invite them so that they have the kind of relationship to God we have?

Think of the people we share activities with—parents of other soccer players, people at work, the neighborhood carpool. Do we know whether these people have a church home? Pray, and rehearse, and commit yourself to invite them to participate in a ministry or attend a service. Don't be pushy. Do it with integrity. Do it in your own voice. Be faithful to yourself and to God. Practice Radical Hospitality. Do it for Christ's sake.

Every member of the Body of Christ is the fruit of someone's ministry and faithfulness. Who is the fruit of yours?

Radical Hospitality. People are searching for churches that make them feel welcome and loved, needed and accepted. The work doesn't stop there. When congregations invite someone to a feast, they can't spend all the time focused on getting the invitations right. They have to consider what will be served. What are they inviting them here for? And this leads to the second practice of vibrant, fruitful, growing congregations: Passionate Worship.

Conversation Questions:

- How do people hear about your church? In what ways are members encouraged to invite and welcome people? How are laity prepared for the work of invitation and hospitality?

- Is there a consistent plan for welcoming visitors who attend worship, children's programs, studies, support groups, and other ministries of the church? What contact do visitors receive and from whom in the first days after visiting? How are they invited to further involvement? How can the practices be improved, better coordinated, and more effective?

- When and where do the laity and clergy of our church receive training each year to enhance hospitality?

- Which groups in your church are the easiest for new people to join? What can your group or class learn from them?

- What is the one activity your group or class could do, which, if done with excellence and consistency, would have the greatest impact on fostering a culture of Radical Hospitality in your congregation?

- How did you become a part of the congregation to which you belong? Describe the services, activities, and people who opened the doors for you. What obstacles made it difficult to feel like you belonged?

- How do you feel about talking to other people about your church? How and when have you invited someone to attend or participate in a ministry of the church?

Group Activity:

Together with other members of your group, walk through the building as if visiting for the first time. Talk about what you see, what you smell, what you hear, what you notice that is welcoming and inviting and helpful, and what you find confusing or uninviting or forbidding. Imagine moving through the building from the point of view of a child, a teenager, a mother with a baby, and a person with a disability.

CHAPTER TWO

THE PRACTICE OF PASSIONATE WORSHIP

"How lovely is your dwelling place, O LORD of hosts! My soul longs, indeed it faints for the courts of the LORD." (Psalm 84:1-2)

1.

Vibrant, fruitful, growing churches offer Passionate Worship that connects people to God and to one another. People gather consciously as the Body of Christ with eagerness and expectancy; encounter Christ through singing, prayer, Scripture, preaching and Holy Communion; and respond by allowing God's Spirit to shape their lives. Lives shaped by God's Spirit become the nucleus for congregations with extraordinary warmth, graciousness, and belonging. People are searching for worship that is authentic, alive, creative, and comprehensible, where they experience the life-changing presence of God in the presence of others.

Once more, we may not ordinarily use the word *passionate* to describe our practice of gathering for worship, but perhaps we should.

Worship describes those times we gather deliberately seeking to encounter God in Christ. We cultivate our relationship with God and with one another as the people of God. We don't attend worship to squeeze God into our

33

lives; we seek to meld our lives into God's. It's a time to think less about ourselves and more about faith, less about our personal agendas and more about God's will. We encounter a fresh vision of God's reality in Christ so that God's Spirit can reshape our lives and form us into the Body of Christ.

Comprehending the meaning of worship requires looking beyond *what people do* to see with the eyes of faith *what God does*. God uses worship to transform lives, heal wounded souls, renew hope, shape decisions, provoke change, inspire compassion, and bind people to one another. God through Christ actively seeks relationship to us through worship.

Through Radical Hospitality, congregations offer the gracious invitation of Christ, open doors to relationship, and foster a sense of belonging. Through Passionate Worship, God draws people to Christ (many for the first time), deepens understanding and relationship with Christ, and over time transforms lives as disciples grow in the image of Christ. God works through the church to make disciples of Jesus Christ, and worship plays an essential role in this process.

From the earliest accounts of faith, people gathered to pray, sing, listen for God's word, and share in the common meal. *Synagogue* means "to bring together," and the Greek word for church, *ekklesia*, means "called out of the"

"Such Belongs to the Kingdom"

A congregation evaluated its volunteer assets and realized it had excellent musical leadership available during the summer among the mothers of young children. It launched a weeklong, on-site music camp for elementary age children. Monday through Friday, children gathered to sing, learn about worship, learn Scripture verses, and practice for a children's musical presentation. After snack lunches, the afternoon included a different fun activity each day, such as swimming, seeing a movie, or taking a trip to the park. On the Sunday following music camp, the children led worship, presenting the musical for the congregation, parents, and the host of visitors who came with extended families. Music camp teaches children songs of the faith, stories of the Bible, and the love of worship!

Another congregation has an acolyte ministry that exceeds all expectations! To participate, children attend interesting classes to learn about worship and to practice how to conduct themselves in their roles of lighting candles and carrying the cross and Bible. The high point of the year is practice, preparation, and participation in one of the church's five Christmas Eve services. More than sixty children play a special part in Christmas Eve services as acolytes! The program creates a desire in children to learn about worship, to lead worship, and to offer their utmost in service to God.

world," and refers to the calling of people from their ordinary life to gather together in sacred time and space. Worship breathes life into the community of Christ's followers, forms identity, and provides a place of common learning about faith and listening to God. People express love for God, serve God, and experience God's gracious love offered freely. Worship forms communities, shapes souls, corrects self-interest, and binds people to each other and to God. God reaches out to us through worship services conducted in traditional and ancient forms or services marked with extraordinary spontaneity. God speaks to us in beautiful sanctuaries and simple buildings, in store-front gathering places and hospital chapels, outdoors under the open sky, and in the homes of members. In every imaginable setting, through worship, people seek to connect with God, allow God's word to shape them, and offer their response of faith. God's Spirit changes us through worship.

Worship was the reason given repeatedly for why God liberated the Hebrew people from slavery in Egypt. "Let my people go, so that they may worship me" (Exodus 8:1). Worship defines God's people.

In worship, people practice the highest command Jesus has taught us: "You shall love the Lord your God with all your heart, and with all your soul, and with all your strength, and with all your mind; and your neighbor as yourself" (Luke 10:27). Worship bends hearts toward God as it stretches hands outward toward others.

Through worship, God pardons sins, restores relationships, and changes lives. Jesus tells the story of the tax collector genuinely and humbly crying to God in the Temple, and says, "I tell you, this man went down to his home justified" (Luke 18:14). Worship is the most likely setting for people to experience the renewed relationship with God that Christians call "justification," in which a person realizes that she or he is pardoned, forgiven, loved, and accepted by God. Teaching the meaning of justification by grace through faith, John Wesley repeatedly reminded early Methodists of how "the new birth" is God's gift-like work in Christ that is received and accepted when people open their hearts to God. Worship is the church's optimum environment for conversion (the return to relationship with God) whether quick, dramatic, and memorable, or marked by gradual shaping and nuanced change over time. God expects lives to change in worship: attendees become disciples of Jesus Christ, and a crowd becomes the Body of Christ.

The Psalmist describes an eagerness for relationship with God in worship, "My soul longs, indeed it faints for the courts of the LORD; my heart and my flesh sing for joy to the living God... For a day in your courts is better than a thousand elsewhere" (Psalm 84:2, 10). Through the relationship to God, cultivated in worship, the psalmist goes "from strength to strength" (Psalm 84:7), receiving the encouragement and daily renewal that characterizes life in God. People practice and experience resurrection in worship; every Sunday is a little Easter.

These definitions describe community worship, a time before God together with other people. Community worship, whether traditional or contemporary, follows implicit consensus of structure, words, actions, pace, and movement. Worship also includes personal devotions, private prayer, meditation, and reading that people practice apart from the physical presence of others in the Body of Christ. Both community worship and personal devotions depend upon each other; they complement and reinforce one another, adding richness to the experience of each.

One pastor described his intention for leading community worship by saying that, in each service, he tries to engage *the intellect* and *the heart* of the worshipers. Through engaging the intellect, worshipers learn something about the content of the faith. They learn about God, Jesus, the stories of Scripture, the practice of the faith, and the world around them. Worship changes minds. Through engaging the heart, he reaches the interior life of worshipers. The intimacy of worship helps them know mercy, grow in hope, sense the Holy Spirit, experience grace, and offer and receive forgiveness. God touches worshipers through music, story, prayer, and communion, and they experience belonging, support, and connection. Worship opens hearts. And finally, the pastor seeks to engage people with a *practical challenge* to do something in their family, community, and world because of their faith in Christ. Worship equips and encourages people and calls them to alter their paths as they grow in Christ-likeness. Worship changes behavior.

2.

If worship includes all of this, why use *passionate* to describe the practices of vibrant, fruitful, growing churches?

Without passion, worship becomes dry, routine, boring, and predictable, keeping the form while lacking the spirit. Insufficient planning by leaders, apathy of worshipers, poor quality music, and unkempt facilities contribute to an experience that people approach with a sense of obligation rather than joy. Interpersonal conflict threatens the life of some congregations, with worshipers and leaders distracted and exhausted by antagonism. Sometimes the service feels like a performance—inauthentic, even self-indulgent, as pastors or music leaders push themselves as the center of attention. Other services include so many announcements, jokes, digressions, and personal stories that have little to do with worship, that the time feels like an informal, loosely-planned, poorly-led meeting. Younger generations and newer Christians find some services incomprehensible because the forms of music, language, and liturgy are so restrained or so foreign. Worship is the most likely point of first contact the unchurched have with a congregation, and in some churches, many visitors do not find genuine warmth, a premium on excellence, or a message presented in a form that engages them. When a congregation loses touch with the purpose of worship, people come and go without receiving God.

To *worship* speaks of devotion to God, the practices that support honor and love of God. *Passionate* describes an intense desire, an ardent spirit, strong feelings, and the sense of heightened importance. *Passionate* speaks of an emotional connection that goes beyond intellectual consent. It connotes eagerness, anticipation, expectancy, deep commitment, and belief.

Passionate Worship means an extraordinary eagerness to offer the best in worship, honoring God with excellence and with an unusual clarity about the purpose of connecting people to God. Whether fifteen hundred people attend, or fifteen, Passionate Worship is alive, authentic, fresh, and engaging. In Passionate Worship, people are honest before God and one another, and open to God's presence, truth, and will for their lives. People so eagerly desire such worship that they will reorder their lives to attend. Searching for wholeness, healing, meaning, connection, restoration, perspective, or hope, people discover that

"Can You Hear Me Now?"

A small rural church with a limited budget had a distracting microphone problem. The pastor's voice would fade in and out, and an annoying popping sound disrupted sermons, prayers, and announcements. The Trustees claimed not to have the money to fix it. One member, frustrated by the fact that the most important gathering time in the congregation's life was constantly being sabotaged and undermined, felt called by God to take personal responsibility to do something. He felt so passionate about worship and believed it was so important to get this fixed that he offered to pay the entire cost himself. Through the frustration of a bad microphone, he heard God calling him to do something so others could hear better and thus enhance the worship experience for all.

when they encounter Christ, their lives are changed and empty places in their spirits are filled up. They attend to learn about Jesus, faith, and life, and they encounter Christ. A warm and compelling sense of belonging appeals to them and makes them feel a part of the Body of Christ. They genuinely look forward to services and invite others to be present with them. For churches that practice Passionate Worship, every effort at preparation provides evidence that this is the most important hour of the week.

In spiritually passionate communities, there's a palpable air of expectancy as people gather for worship. Musicians, ushers, greeters, and other hosts arrive early, and with care and eagerness they prepare together, encouraging one another. They genuinely delight in one another's presence, and they give attention to the smallest of details to make the service go well for worshipers. The gathering congregation, even when it includes many first-time visitors, never feels like a crowd of strangers. There's a unifying anticipation, a gracious and welcoming texture to the way people speak, act, and prepare. Clearly, the pastor, music leaders, and worshipers expect something important to take place, and they're eager to be part of it. They expect God to speak to them while they experience God's presence, forgiveness, hope, or direction. Singing together, joining voices in prayer, listening to the Word, confessing sins, celebrating the sacraments, they intermingle their lives with each other, and they connect to God. Expectancy pervades the congregation, the active passion to serve God and to love one another. You can feel it.

Many times we unconsciously enter worship in the evaluative posture of someone preparing a movie critique. We rate the sermon, the time for children, the prayers, and the music according to some internal scale. "How was the service? Well, the sermon was too long, the piano too loud, the children too noisy, and the room too cold." Our attention turns to the imperfections, mispronunciations, missed cues, discordant sounds, personal discomforts, and the weaknesses of the leaders and flaws of fellow worshipers.

In a mind-set of expectancy, as opposed to one of searching for every human weakness, worshipers discover that God wants a relationship with them and seeks to say something through the time together. People are not at worship to observe and evaluate but to receive what God offers and offer their best in response. "What is God saying to me through the words of Scripture, even if they are read imperfectly; through the sermon, even if the illustrations are weak; and through the unifying power of music, even if the organist drags the pace a little? What does God say that we need to hear through the prayer, the creed, and the sacrament of Holy Communion? Am I allowing God's Spirit to form me, change me, transform me through these experiences, or am I evaluating the quality of entertainment?"

Passionate Worship connects people with God and with one another, opens lives to the experience of God's grace and to the hearing and doing of God's Word, and forms people into the Body of Christ. Passionate Worship is not performance, nor is it mechanical motions, merely gathering because it's eleven o'clock on Sunday morning. A passionate spiritual community is alive with the love of God, displaying an eagerness for God's word.

Passionate Worship is not restricted to any particular style; it can be highly formal, with robes, acolytes, stained glass, organ music, orchestral accompaniment, and hardwood pews with hymnals on the rack in front. Or Passionate Worship can take place in an auditorium, gym, or storefront, with casually dressed leaders, images on screens, folding chairs, and the supporting beat of a praise team. Authentic, engaging, life-changing worship derives from the experience of God's presence, the desire of worshipers for God's word, and the changed heart people deliberately seek when they encounter Christ in the presence of other Christians. Worship leaves people challenged, sustained, and led by the Spirit of God, and it changes how they view themselves and their neighbors. An hour of Passionate Worship changes all the other hours of the week.

The regular practice of Passionate Worship gives people an interpretive lens through which to view the world, helping them see events, relationships, and issues through God's eyes. Among the competing interpretive contexts in which people are immersed (fierce individualism, acquisitive consumerism, intense nationalism, political partisanship, hopeless negativism, naïve optimism) worship helps people perceive themselves, their world, their relationships, and their responsibilities in ways that include God's revelation in Christ. The language of the Spirit (love, grace, joy, hope, forgiveness, compassion, justice, community) provides people the means to express interior experience and relational aspirations. Stories of faith (Scripture, parable, testimony) deepen perception and meaning. The practices of worship (singing, praying, the sacraments) rehearse connection to God and to others. Under the influence of weekly worship, people practice looking at the world in a different way and rehearse their unique calling as people of God and their unique identity as the Body of

Christ. Worship changes people and changes the way they experience their whole lives.

Churches aspiring to have Passionate Worship work hard to deepen spiritual life and improve the quality of worship to help connect people to God. They make worship appealing and accessible while deepening theological integrity. Poor quality robs worship of its power and purpose.

The pastors of a certain large congregation decided worship had grown stale and routine. Worshipers were not complaining, and attendance was strong. But to the staff, worship had slipped to a lower priority as each staff member moved mechanically through her or his assigned role with little creativity or sense of purpose. The staff, including pastors, youth director, musicians, sound system operator, secretary, nursery director, and volunteer coordinator of ushers, planned a day together to focus on the principal worship service. One of the pastors hosted the day at her home, and the "mini-retreat" began early in the morning and continued until late afternoon. They evaluated every element of the service and discussed why they do what they do in the way they do it. They considered alternatives and reflected on the theological meanings of their choices. They discussed how each element of worship connects people to God and to each other, and how it could be improved. The gathering, the prelude and the announcements, how and when pastors and choirs enter and exit, and where people stand and how they move—all came under review. They considered the length, content, purpose, and placement of every action, discussing tone, atmosphere, and pace. Imagining the perspective of long-term members, newcomers, children, and parents with young children, they reviewed lines of sight, eye contact, lighting, and sound. They discussed who led what portions of the service and why, and where the staff greeted people before and after the service. They talked about giving more attention to their own spiritual preparation to avoid moving through the service by rote.

These conversations resulted in several changes, some simple and barely noticeable, others affecting texture and tone, and a few altering the service order. They consolidated announcements into one time at the beginning, eliminating the interruptions that broke the prayerful, reflective mood later in the service. They reduced small talk and distracting digressions between movements while keeping an invitational and gracious quality. They smoothed transitions to improve pace, removing gaps that gave the impression that someone had forgotten what to do. They expanded the pastoral prayer to include more expressions connecting the congregation to the world, specifically to those who suffer from disease, hunger, or the violence of war, and they added silent prayer to deepen the sense of unity and awe. They came to consensus about how to use images on the screen, and limited distracting changes in lighting. They solved communications problems between musicians and pastors so that announcements, prelude, and entries flowed more smoothly. Minor seating adjustments removed visually distracting movements behind the preacher during sermons. They agreed upon language to introduce the offering to reinforce the theological underpinnings of tithing, and they developed a consistent way to welcome people into membership at the close of the service. The usher coordinator and nursery director worked on a plan to handle restless children with graciousness.

What changed as a result of this thorough review? The content of the service actually changed little, but the quality, pace, movement, and connection with the people improved dramatically. Pastors and staff worked with renewed creativity and purpose. Worship leaders improved communication among themselves. The experience was so positive and fruitful that the staff held another retreat to focus on the contemporary service, and then another to review services of Holy Communion.

More than anything else, the quality of spiritual preparation of the worship leaders improved. It was obvious that the pastors and staff were praying, reading, preparing, and offering their best. The pastors considered worship vitally important, worthy of their highest efforts, and this passion in the leaders shaped how other members viewed worship. Staff were inviting worshipers to join them in a spiritual journey, an adventure of faith, with the expectation of God's continuing presence. By reminding themselves of the purpose of worship, the staff no longer moved routinely through the motions. Worship came alive again for them, and for the congregation.

When worship becomes a high priority, Passionate Worship is evident, and it shows in everything worship leaders do. They regularly evaluate and rethink their patterns of worship with an eye toward creative engagement and the spiritual progress of the congregation.

One small congregation approached the renewal of worship differently from the way in which the large congregation reviewed its worship. The pastor, volunteer organist, and a few members met to plan what to do to deepen the worship life of the church. They spent an evening discussing the purpose of worship. They studied Scripture, prayed, read a chapter in a book about worship, and came to the conclusion that Christian worship is "for the love of God." Then they conscientiously considered what each person might do "for the love of God" to make Sunday worship more special. They humbly opened themselves to creative change.

One member volunteered to place fresh-cut flowers in the chancel each Sunday, a dramatic improvement over the plastic ones. This she would do "for the love of God." Another member volunteered to arrive early each Sunday "for the love of God" and go through the small sanctuary, wiping dust from the furnishings, arranging the hymnals, and cleaning up so that the sanctuary looked inviting and smelled fresh. The pastor, prompted graciously by some of the members, decided that "for the love of God" he would prepare less formal sermons and work on preaching with more eye contact and a more relaxed posture. He'd try to make the sermons more practical and useful for people. They decided that "for the love of God" they would close each service with everyone (about thirty people) holding hands for prayer. They decided "for the love of God" to take communion to the homebound whenever they celebrated the sacrament and that "for the love of God" they would talk to the Trustees about making the entry handicapped accessible. "For the love of God," the organist even agreed to support the soloist in singing with recorded music from time to time!

These little changes, appropriate to a small family-sized congregation, reveal how much the people care about worship, that it really matters to them, and that they really believe something is at stake in this sacred time. When people passionately care about worship and expect to encounter God in these moments together, it changes how they behave in preparation for it. Churches cannot expect visitors and members to take worship seriously if they do not act as if it is important to them. What can we do to improve our worship as a congregation? How can passionate love of God help contribute to worship that is alive, engaging, authentic, appealing, creative, and theologically sound?

3.

Passionate Worship is contextual, an expression of the unique culture of a congregation. Communities have their own distinct patterns, voice, and language for loving God authentically. Cultural nuances, regional practices, denominational particularities, theological leanings, pastoral preferences, congregational size and age, and preferred styles (such as traditional, contemporary, praise, or emerging church) shape worship practices in diverse ways.

Even with a thousand distinctive ways to worship, congregations marked by the quality of Passionate Worship stand apart. Worship is alive, engaging, appealing, and life changing, and leaders take seriously the importance of spiritual and practical preparation. People recognize that pastors and musicians love God and love worship. Leaders are clear about the purpose of connecting people to God and of God's desire to form people into the Body of Christ. In whatever culture or context, Passionate Worship includes the "aha" moments that change people and mold them, the touch of transcendence that pulls them out of themselves, deepens their understanding of life and their relationship to God, and makes them feel richer, stronger, and truer to what God has created them to be.

Many churches offer less formal worship, singing praise music supported by guitar, percussion, and keyboard; relying upon screens for the words; and having leaders who dress casually and speak without a pulpit or notes. These services connect to some people of all ages more effectively than formal services do.

But an increased tempo and volume of music, more visual stimulation, and less formality in speaking and dressing do not mean a congregation succeeds in connecting people to God and allowing God to form them into the Body of Christ. As contradictory as it sounds, churches that practice Passionate Worship in a contemporary style work diligently at their spontaneity. When pursuing excellence in music and message, they coordinate the message between musicians and preachers, they evaluate every movement to maximize effect, they immerse their preparation in prayer, and they restrain the temptation to form self-indulgent personality cults around

---

"Worship Shaped by the Context"

When Meri Whitaker was assigned to Canterbury Chapel in the Oklahoma Indian Missionary Conference, the congregation had dwindled to a small group of older, highly committed women. They worked and prayed for some way to bring others into the life of the church. Immersing herself in the community, the pastor came to realize the dramatic need for Twelve-Step support groups based on the Alcoholics Anonymous recovery model. The congregation decided to take a risk and adapted their worship to complement and support the twelve steps. The worship service became a powerful center for testimony, decision, support, and transformation. The congregation now averages over a hundred people each week. Few United Methodist congregations are as acutely aware of the life-transforming power of worship as Canterbury Chapel.

gifted musicians or pastors. They work together as a team with a clear focus on their purpose. They remember that the service is not about them but about God and that serving God requires everyone's best. Each service includes ordinary elements that remain the same from week to week, lending stability, predictability, and constancy. And each service includes elements that change, especially within the music, the message, and the visual support. Spontaneity is planned with a clear purpose in mind. Worship leaders make it look so easy precisely because they work so hard.

A congregation that offered a single traditional Sunday morning service with about 300 in attendance decided to launch a contemporary service aimed at attracting and involving younger people. They consulted with other churches that had successfully launched similar services, sent visitors to other contemporary services, recruited a music team mostly from among their own congregation, and began planning with musicians, worship leaders, and with the volunteers to operate sound and video. The pastor, more comfortable with traditional worship, sought coaching from colleagues who had made similar transitions. She decided to preach the same content as she preached for the traditional service but in a less formal teaching mode, using screens to highlight Scripture and key points. A core group of members committed to attend for a season, and the church publicized the new service and launched it in January to take advantage of high attendance during that time of year and to benefit from publicity during Christmas services and programs.

Three years later, attendance at the traditional service averages 275, and attendance at the contemporary service has grown to a consistent 135. What has the churched learned through this successful experience? First, the new service calls forth people and uses gifts that the traditional service never did. Many musicians who give hours to the weekly preparation of the new service were only nominally active in church before. Second, more middle-aged and older adults attend the service than young people, and young people continue to attend the traditional service in similar numbers as before. Third, the relaxed, open, informal style requires hard work, good communication, and excellent cooperation to achieve a coherent message. Fourth, the effectiveness and integrity of the contemporary service derives from the high-quality talent, spiritual maturity, and cooperative disposition of the musicians. Finally, success depends upon the active support and encouragement of long-time members, musicians, and church leaders who never attend the new service and who have no taste for contemporary styles.

Of primary significance is the last point. Overall worship attendance increased by more than 100 weekly, and more people connect to God through worship than ever before. Key to the success is the verbal support, visible permission, and unequivocal encouragement of church leaders and musicians who never attend the new service! They launched a fruitful new service that is changing lives, and they avoided the "worship wars" that sabotage many new efforts.

Worship wars erupt when church leaders force a dramatic change of style in music and liturgy upon an existing service. Nobody can make country-and-western fans enjoy rap music, or rock 'n' rollers appreciate Mozart. Nor can traditional organists, choir members, and worshipers be forced to give up the music and liturgy that has helped them connect to God their whole life. Traditional worship forms and music can be improved, enhanced, and deepened in a thousand ways, but people cannot be forced to change their taste in music.

Churches avoid this first kind of conflict by starting another service that does not require current members to sacrifice their style of worship. Or they gently blend music styles in the existing service to allow a wider range of people to find their spiritual needs addressed. Many vibrant, fruitful, growing congregations offer blended services that touch the hearts of diverse worshipers in ways that unify and strengthen the congregation.

Worship wars also ensue when church leaders initiate an alternative service but traditionalist worshipers and musicians refuse to give their blessing to the efforts. "They'll kill our existing service. Microphone stands, drum sets, and video screens ruin the sacred feel. Christian pop entertainment is not worship. They rob good singers from the traditional choir." It's amazing how good Christian folk vociferously and antagonistically resist launching a service they don't plan to attend anyway! It's not intended for them, and to sabotage the desire for worship of those who have different tastes is like unreasonable diners demanding that their favorite restaurant refuse to serve chicken to anyone, anytime, forever, because they prefer beef!

Alleviating this second kind of conflict requires an unusual spiritual maturity among the long-term members. They must show a willingness to support forms of ministry that they do not personally appreciate.

An older gentlemen, his eyes watery with emotion, said, "I'd do anything to have my children and grandchildren in church again. They've lost touch with the faith. The church means everything to me, and it breaks my heart that my own family members don't attend anywhere." A friend responded, "You'd do anything? Would you change your taste in music?" He answered without hesitation, "I can't do that!"

Maybe people can't change their taste in music. But to reach younger generations, churches may need to offer worship in a variety of forms with a diversity of music and perhaps with more images than words. Supporting innovative styles of worship requires a spiritual maturity, a willingness to set aside long-standing tastes and preferences to encourage other people's quest for God.

Flexibility to change the way of presenting God's Word runs through the United Methodist heritage. John Wesley stretched himself beyond his own traditional tastes and practices and, in his own words, "submitted to be more vile" (*Journal*, April 2, 1739) when he began to preach outdoors in fields to reach those beyond the church's touch. Wesley kept the end in mind—helping people find a way to God and helping God find a way to people—even if it required forms he himself found distasteful. Thank God for his spiritual maturity and liturgical agility! Our rich heritage of worship comes to us through many convolutions of style and practice. Outdoor camp meetings, frontier revivals, high-church liturgies, African-American spirituals—these are but a few of many streams of passionate religious practice that flow through our history.

A hundred years ago, a congregation had three generations present in worship, and all spoke the same language, shared the same culture, grew up with the same stories, and enjoyed the same style of music. Now congregations include four or more generations, and each has its own preferred way of communicating, its own distinctive tastes in music, its own language and culture. Have you ever watched a Super Bowl ad that a company spent millions of dollars to produce, and after thirty seconds still had no idea what product they were advertising? That means the ad wasn't intended for you. It was aimed at another generational niche. Ask your grandchildren, and they'll tell you what the ad was for!

Congregations must work hard to speak the language, engage the culture, and use the voice, music, and methods that offer authentic and effective worship experiences for younger generations. In many churches, the elected leadership and the people with the greatest influence and resources still prefer more traditional forms. If they only support worship that suits their own tastes and speaks to their own niche, the church fails to reach younger generations. Vibrant, fruitful, growing congregations succeed because spiritually mature and passionate leaders visibly support and encourage worship and music in diverse forms and expressions. They keep the end in mind, helping people find a way to God by making God's gracious message available in worship.

Passion is evident in these examples: the staff for whom worship deserves an entire day apart to evaluate, a church whose leadership pursues excellence "for the love of God," and a congregation that navigates the perilous cross-currents of conflicting worship preferences to offer two styles of worship with faithfulness and excellence. In each case, people love worship and pour their time and creativity into improving, strengthening, and excelling. That's the quality of Passionate Worship that characterizes vibrant, fruitful, growing congregations

When I visit a church as a bishop to preach, consecrate a building, or confirm a class of young people, I learn much about the pastor's and congregation's standard for excellence. Usually they've gone to considerable effort to prepare the facility, plan the service, and offer special music. I see churches at their best, yet I wonder what worship is like on Sundays when there are no announced special guests.

If none of the worship leaders know who does what or where to stand and sit; or the communion table is littered with hymnals, a cigarette lighter, a Styrofoam cup and a stack of music sheets; or half the lights above the chancel are burnt out; or the choir doesn't know the music, and the organist doesn't realize she's playing too loud; or we're attempting hymns that no one knows or enjoys; or the microphones whistle and crackle and whine and hiss; or the ushers talk out loud at the back and move down the aisles with little cards in their hands counting heads during the prayer; or the praise team leader introduces a song with an off-color joke; or choir members work crossword puzzles during Communion; or the music director and pastor refuse to speak to each other; or the pastor insists on telling a long, self-indulgent and self-congratulatory story before the offering; then what am I to conclude about the pastor's and congregation's standard of excellence? And what am I to imagine worship is like when the bishop is *not* present?

All churches offer worship services. Passionate Worship means a church cares enough about the service to offer its best, its utmost, its highest. Churches that practice Passionate Worship make this sacred time as free as possible from distractions, annoyances, and inconveniences, and people sense the deliberate care in preparation and intention. They leave behind grievances, interpersonal rifts, the need for attention, and the desire to control, and they love God with all their heart and soul and strength and mind. By simple acts, lovingly offered, churches with Passionate Worship draw people to God and to one another in Christ's name, and they afford people the opportunity to be shaped by God.

4.

What difference does the practice of Passionate Worship make?

Worship leaders and pastors who evidence Passionate Worship not only put their best efforts into preparing for their own distinct responsibilities, but they also intentionally work together with others who lead the service. They encourage one another and communicate with each other so that the service progresses smoothly with a unified sense of direction and purpose, with each element of the service building upon another, creating a sense of anticipation about what comes next. They pray together and plan together to make the service cohesive and effective, and worshipers see the spirit of cooperation.

Passionate Worship motivates pastors not only to improve their preaching but also to learn continually how to enhance content and technique for effective worship. They discuss and evaluate and learn from each other in pursuit of excellence; they read books and articles together with the staff; they attend workshops on preaching, music, and technique; they search the internet and subscribe to services for resources; and they visit other churches. They pray earnestly for discernment and open themselves to God's Word and the Spirit's guidance. Worship is something alive that requires continuing care, cultivation, and

"Something New for Christmas"

One congregation had been offering the same menu of Christmas Eve services for decades: an early evening service with Communion, and a late evening candlelight and carols service with high church music (mostly in Latin and German) that ended at midnight. The Communion services were sparsely attended but highly valued by church members, and the late service was well-attended but seldom included many children because of the lateness of the hour. The church staff, after years of offering the same services, suddenly realized how few young families were attending on Christmas Eve. The formality of the Communion service made parents hesitate to bring their children, and many members had family guests with them on Christmas eve from other denominations who were reluctant to attend Communion for their own denominational reasons.

effort to keep it fresh. Pastors willingly review and evaluate their own work and invite feedback. They love worship and long to offer their best to the glory of God and for building the Body of Christ.

Passionate spiritual communities not only worship and pray at Sunday services, they also make worship an essential element of every mission trip, youth program, adult retreat, capital funds campaign, and ministry initiative. They immerse the work of the church in prayer. They not only invite women and men to serve on worship planning teams, but they also develop lay people who feel competent and comfortable in leading prayers for choirs, classes, kitchen crews, work teams, and hospital visits. Members volunteer devotions for Advent, Lent, the newsletter, the website, or special programs. Worship and

After considerable conversation and planning, the staff decided to offer an early evening candlelight service designed for families, fifty minutes in length with blended styles of music. Immediately following this service, they offered a half-hour quiet, formal service of Communion for anyone desiring to remain and for anyone showing up especially for the sacrament. They continued to offer the late night service unchanged. In the first year, total attendance for Christmas Eve more than doubled, and the attendance in years since has doubled again. Most of the early evening worshipers are young families with children, bringing their extended families and providing an abundance of visitors and unchurched people with a positive experience of worship. Those who value Christmas Eve Communion still receive it, and the late formal service continues to remain strong with roughly the same attendance it has enjoyed for many years. Thankfully, the staff and congregation cared enough about worship to rethink, risk change, and develop new traditions that better serve the changing context and styles of younger worshipers.

prayer led by the laity become natural and expected. These churches don't stop at *encouraging* people to pray at home; they *teach* people to pray, offering classes, studies, and retreats; and they provide quality resources for private devotions, such as *The Upper Room Disciplines* or self-published collections written by members. They take seriously the Wesleyan disciplines of daily personal prayer and Scripture reading, the frequent receiving of the Holy Communion, and occasional fasting—practices through which God shapes the soul and forms disciples. Private devotion reinforces common worship. Spiritual communities pray without ceasing.

In churches that practice Passionate Worship, the music is at least good, usually excellent, but never mediocre. Music speaks directly to the soul, setting the tone and the emotional texture of the service. In some congregations, music may be simple, but it is dynamic, inspirational, and high quality. Music moves people, unifies congregations, strengthens the sense of belonging, provokes reflection, inspires joy, and lifts the spirit. Passionate worshiping communities place a premium on excellence and invite to leadership positions musicians with outstanding talent who understand that the purpose of music in worship is to connect people to God. Choirs and praise teams offer their work as ministry, they care for one another and pray for one another, and they hone their talent to the glory of God. Quality music resonates through congregations who emphasize Passionate Worship.

Services that reflect passion for worship are balanced, using a mixture of complex and simple elements to communicate the message, a rhythm ranging from fast-paced and upbeat to reflective and quiet, and a tone that varies from graciously lighthearted and winsome to serious and respectful. Variation speaks both to heart and mind, and addresses those who prefer linear verbal progression as well as others who learn through images, metaphors, and stories. When possible, significant spiritual leadership from both male and female leaders helps connect to a greater diversity of people. And Passionate Worship addresses more than one or two of the five senses, going beyond listening to words. Movement during sacraments, the offering, and the time for children engages worshipers. Silence as well as song deepens unity and reverence. Visual focal points draw peoples' eyes toward a cross or communion table. The bread tastes good and smells newly-baked, flowers are fresh, and candles glow with real flames. In traditional sanctuaries, stained glass retells the stories of faith, and the building's architecture lifts the eyes and heart. In contemporary services, well-lit screens show images carefully selected to supplement the purpose of the service and not to detract from it. Worship leaders control the content to support the message and tone of the service. Periods of greeting encourage people to shake hands so everyone feels the touch of others, and in some churches, worshipers hold hands during prayer. Passionate worshiping communities enliven aesthetic sensibilities to the beauty of God, giving worshipers multifaceted pathways to the truth of Christ. Worship is approachable, accessible, and comprehensible to the people that passionate worshiping communities seek to serve.

In churches marked by Passionate Worship, people don't merely show up and sit passively in their pews; they are actively engaged, genuinely connected, personally addressed, and deeply challenged. The message touches them, the music moves them, and the service changes them.

People make spiritual progress, they want to be present, and they approach worship with a sense of expectancy, anticipating God's presence. They talk about their experiences to others, invite their friends, and view worship as the most important hour of the week for themselves and for the church.

Pastors who lead Passionate Worship actively nurture their own spiritual lives. Authenticity and integrity derive from their personal practice of faith. They worship *with* others as they lead worship *for* others, and their public prayers find their source in genuine spiritual disciplines. Congregations detect whether a pastor goes through the motions pro forma, preparing an act or a performance in a perfunctory manner, or whether his or her message and expression derive from a growing faith and love for God and people. Pastors who cultivate Passionate Worship demonstrate adaptability, a willingness to learn new ways to serve people. They don't appear stuck, resistant, or rigid, and they don't insist on their own way when their personal preferences fail to serve the congregation's spiritual progress.

When churches practice Passionate Worship, the gathering forms a congregation that is a community and not a crowd of people experiencing the same thing like strangers at a movie. People feel welcomed and supported; they sense belonging, mutual affection, warmth, and connection. There is a self-conscious awareness, even if unspoken, that God is fashioning these people into the Body of Christ. Visitors and the unchurched form impressions through their experience of worship. They look for openness to belonging. "Do they love one another? Will they love me? Is God active in this community? Is there evidence of God's grace in how they treat each other?" Passionate worshiping congregations appeal to newcomers because people delight in one another and feel grateful in being together. Visitors choose a community in which they learn, find hope and help, and are warmly and graciously welcomed from the time they arrive in the parking lot until they leave to return home.

Congregations that practice Passionate Worship experience the sacraments of Holy Baptism and Holy Communion as means of grace, ways by which God actively forms disciples and builds the Body of Christ. Rather than merely performing an act of Christian cuteness, they view infant baptism as initiation into the Body of Christ, an expression of the unmerited gracious initiative of God's love. They instruct parents with care, assist the whole church in understanding the significance of baptism, and take time to make the symbols come alive for people of all ages. Pastors leading Passionate Worship don't read through the Communion liturgy in a mundane and perfunctory fashion as if the point is to get it over with. They engage people with the words, the story, and the symbols through inflection, pause, emphasis, voice, tone, and movement. They practice until they feel confident and familiar with the liturgy, they learn to perform the rubrics smoothly, and they respect the mystery and awe of the sacrament while making it appealing and accessible. They do not lead Communion spiritually unprepared or without paying attention to details. Their manner of serving Communion is not impersonal or mechanical; they engage people with graciousness and humility. Their own passion, respect, and love of the sacrament pervade the service, inviting people into the sacred sharing of bread and cup.

Churches that practice Passionate Worship place special emphasis on Christmas Eve and Easter Sunday services, knowing the disproportionate opportunity these services offer for the church to touch the lives of visitors and nominal members. They make the music, message, and liturgy more accessible than ever to those with limited knowledge of the faith. Visitors and extended family members feel welcomed and supported in their participation rather than self-conscious about their unfamiliarity with the church. They naturally interweave the practice of Radical Hospitality with Passionate Worship, welcoming new people so God's love can touch them and transform them. In addition to Easter and Christmas, spiritually passionate congregations plan one or two exceptionally high quality, widely-publicized special services per year that feature a guest preacher, launch a mission initiative, present a children's musical, or culminate a stewardship campaign. For these special events, they go to extraordinary measures to invite people, writing personal letters or forming phone committees. Widely attended special services strengthen the sense of belonging and identity, reinvigorate infrequent worshipers, and attract visitors.

Worship leaders who care passionately about worship not only review and coordinate their roles and responsibilities thirty minutes before the service begins, they also communicate early in the week so everyone has time to prepare and to offer his or her best to a unified effort. Staff and volunteers tend to details, fix sound problems, adjust the lighting, clean carpet stains, and replace candles on Thursdays or Fridays rather than immediately before the service begins as the congregation gathers.

Churches that exhibit passion for worship prepare their services not only with long-term, spiritually mature members in mind but also with attentiveness to visitors, young people, and those with little worship experience in mind. There is an open quality to every element of the service, making it easy and appealing for people to participate, become involved, and connect. Their worship displays Radical Hospitality. Handouts, announcements, and signs are free of insider language and acronyms; prayers, creeds, and liturgical responses are printed so that newcomers don't feel like confused and ignorant outsiders. Elements of the service engage children, or children's church is provided, so that young people can learn to worship and to pray. During every service, pastors offer an invitation to further discipleship or membership, and they encourage visitors to engage in personal conversation with staff members or volunteers to learn more about getting involved in church life. Everything says, "We're glad you're here. Come back. Learn more. We'll help."

5.

God in Christ changes people's lives through Passionate Worship. Worship stirs people's souls, inspires them, and strengthens them. They find such help and courage and belonging and care that they cannot help but talk about the sermons, ideas, stories, music, and prayers during the week. "I am the vine," Jesus said, and "you are the branches" (John 15:5). Worship connects the branches to the vine, keeps people connected to the source of life, and helps them grow in Christ. Worshipers who are absent feel that they have missed something, and they also feel missed. Passionate spiritual communities increase in attendance because members and visitors cannot help but talk positively about their experiences with others. There's a contagious quality to authentic, engaging worship, to relevant sermons and uplifting music and warm community. Just as in the early church, God adds to their number day by day because worshipers naturally invite those with whom they have other things in common, bearing witness to the helpfulness, insight, and spiritual sustenance they've found. Passionate Worship supports and nourishes all other ministries, missions, and outreach of the congregation, giving life, vision, direction, and encouragement to the whole Body of Christ.

Offering their best and highest efforts, pastors, musicians, and worship leaders play an essential role as they pursue excellence through prayerful planning, spiritual preparation, and constant learning. But the responsibility for worship rests with more than those who lead the services. *Everyone* has a role in fostering Passionate Worship.

Imagine a church deciding to enhance the congregation's worship life, asking each ministry area and committee, each Sunday school and Bible study, each staff member and choir to do something extra "for the love of God" to strengthen community worship and deepen the practice of personal devotions.

Imagine the Trustees reviewing with the pastor the functionality and effectiveness of microphones, sound systems, and lighting, and looking through the chancel, sanctuary, foyer, and nursery to see that these places look fresh, inviting, clean, safe, and well-lit. Does the way people care for their place of worship reveal their passion for worship and their love for God?

Imagine mission teams, work project leaders, and volunteer coordinators intentionally including periods of prayer, devotion, worship, or Communion with their groups. The church might launch a congregation-wide prayer ministry that interweaves the petitions, intercessions, and thanksgivings of members and visitors for the strengthening of the Body of Christ and the ministry of the church. Those with an interest in writing and a familiarity with computer publishing might print seasonal devotional collections, soliciting volunteers to compose meditations, and distributing them so that members are reading and praying the same material at the same time.

Imagine the women of the church planning an overnight Lenten or Advent retreat at a hotel, guest house, or retreat center to focus on prayer or other spiritual disciplines. The children's ministry planners might begin an acolyte program that goes beyond lighting candles to include teachings on prayer and worship. The men's group might provide transportation for housebound members to worship or develop a recording ministry that delivers copies of the service to homebound members. The Communications Committee might review the content and style of the bulletin, place ads for special services in the newspaper, and refresh the appearance of the church newsletter to emphasize worship as the central activity of the church.

Imagine the Staff-Parish Relations Committee discussing how to foster learning opportunities and adequate spiritual preparation for the pastor and staff to support excellence in worship. How does the church support their participation at workshops and seminars on worship and preaching, and how does it encourage them to visit other congregations with quality authentic worship so that the church benefits from the collaborative learning of pastors, musicians, and staff?

Imagine ushers, greeters, nursery personnel, and other hosts meeting together to pray and discuss how to deepen the quality of warmth and hospitality so that it exceeds all expectations for visitors and members alike.

Just imagine if each committee and work team and staff member focused on enhancing worship. Perhaps no one thing would improve by 100 percent. But maybe a hundred things would improve by 1 percent, and the passionate love of God evidenced in these changes would renew congregational life.

The responsibility for the quality of spiritual life in the congregation does not reside only with the pastor. And committees and teams and staff can't do it on their own, either. What each person brings to worship shapes the experience for everyone as much as what he or she finds there. Passionate Worship begins with each worshiping individual.

One way to deepen the experience of worship is for each person to actively prepare his or her heart, mind, and soul before attending. Nothing reinforces the practice of prayer and learning from Scripture better than a vibrant personal devotional life. Many churches publish Scriptures or topics before services so that members can review the readings, meditate on the verses, and prepare for worship. Other churches encourage members to take notes, or they provide a sermon outline so that people can rethink the key points at home after services. How do you prepare your heart, mind, and soul for worship?

Another way for each person to enhance the worship life of a congregation is to help create the sense of warmth and welcome that helps others feel they belong. No one should attend worship without feeling the welcome of Christ. How do you influence an atmosphere of genuine care and belonging for others?

Worship soars on the God-given gifts of congregational members. Do you offer yourself and your best to sing or to serve as usher or greeter or reader? Are you willing to learn and teach about prayer in your Sunday School class, youth ministry, or Bible study?

Our experience of worship begins with the attitude, the spiritual eagerness, and passion we bring with us. *The United Methodist Hymnal* (p. vii) includes John Wesley's "Directions for Singing" from 1761. He encouraged the early Methodists to "sing lustily and with good courage. Be aware of singing as if you are half dead or half asleep, but lift your voice in strength...Above all, sing spiritually. Have an eye to God in every word you sing. Aim at pleasing him more than yourself, or any other creature." In how we sing and pray, in how we greet others, in how we approach the sacraments, Passionate Worship begins with our love for God, our desire to open ourselves to God's grace, and our eagerness for relationship to God. What kind of attitude and eagerness do you bring with you to worship?

People come to worship carrying many concerns. Some worry about a cousin serving in the military; others face financial struggles that tear at the fabric of family life. Some sense a disturbing lack of fulfillment in their careers, fear health challenges, or feel deeply affected by the immensity of a distant tragedy. Some face monumental decisions while others must constantly moderate intense conflict at home. Some are overwhelmed with gratitude, humbled by feelings of love and joy, or seeking discernment on how to channel their charitable impulses. Every congregation, large and small, is a tapestry of hope and hurt, a collage of experience and anticipation, a patchwork quilt of gifts, needs, fears, and aspirations. People come to connect to God and one another as well as to feel restored, reminded, remembered, and refreshed. They wonder what God has to do with all that's going on inside of them and in the world around them. They want to know that having a relationship with Christ changes their life. In their searching, God finds them, heals them, sustains them, and forms them anew.

The motivation for enhancing the quality of worship is not only about deepening our own faith but also about allowing God to use us and our congregations to offer hope and life and love to others. God works through us to change the world. Worship is God's gift and task, a sacred trust that requires our utmost and highest.

Engagement with the Body of Christ depends upon the gracious, inviting quality of Radical Hospitality. The spiritual vitality of a congregation results from viewing Passionate Worship as the essential gathering of the people of God and as a place where God changes hearts, redeems souls, and transforms lives. But the spiritual progress of a congregation and its members depends on more than what happens during a weekly period of worship. This takes us to the next practice of vibrant, fruitful, growing congregations: Intentional Faith Development.

Conversation Questions:

- How does the congregation encourage the pastor, staff, laity, and musicians who lead worship to give adequate time to the preparation of sermons and music so as to enhance excellence? When and where do worship leaders receive training? How does the congregation encourage and support training for worship leaders?
- How does the congregation make children feel welcome in worship? How does the youth ministry of the church include significant worship experiences and participation?
- In what ways does your class or group practice and teach prayer? How do you pray for one another, for the church, and for the needs of the world?
- What practices, readings, resources, or relationships sustain your own personal devotional life? How do you prepare your own spirit for worship?

Group Activity:

Arrange for several of your class members who have never done so to sit in the chancel or choir loft during an entire worship service. Then ask them about what they noticed or learned about the practice of worship or about the congregation as it worships. How does sitting up front change their perception of worship?

CHAPTER THREE

THE PRACTICE OF INTENTIONAL FAITH DEVELOPMENT

"They devoted themselves to the apostles' teaching and fellowship, to the breaking of bread and the prayers." (Acts 2:42)

1.

In a remote village a half-day's walk outside of Jerusalem, a woman fed dried branches into a fire as she prepared to make bread for the day. She dipped her hands into the water of a small basin that sat beside the vase she had carried from the well before sunrise. She sighed deeply at the prospect of another day of unending work just to scrape enough food together to feed her daughters and herself. Since her husband's sudden illness and death, she had felt abandoned and alone in ways she could barely fathom. As she felt the cool water trickle through her fingers, she thought about the story she had heard the night before as she gathered with her neighbors for prayer and supper. It was a story about a woman who met Jesus at a well, where he talked about "living water." She also remembered the story someone told about Jesus touching the man who had been paralyzed for so long. Then a stream of stories cascaded through her mind, tumbling one into another. She thought about a shepherd and his sheep and a woman and her coin, two women's tears of sorrow and joy before an empty tomb, and a poor widow giving more than all the rich people in the Temple. She smiled to herself thinking about that last one.

She had heard about Jesus for the first time only a few months earlier, and now his stories were hers. Word spread about his horrible death (he had been only a couple of years older than her husband when he had died), and then, amazingly, about his being alive and about his followers gathering first in Jerusalem and then here and there in other villages. There were stories of Jesus spoken in the Temple that were retold in the streets and talked about in the homes among her friends. She began to listen, and what she heard amazed her. And the people who told the stories invited her into their homes. *Her. Into their homes.* She could hardly believe it. Everyone knew that without a husband, she was on her own, destitute. But these people treated her differently. She and her daughters ate with them, receiving more than they could ever repay. And they prayed *for* her and *with* her for her daughters. This unexpected love changed everything in her life. Suddenly she didn't feel abandoned and alone; she felt connected and loved, like her life counted for something. Then she couldn't get enough of the stories or of her friends, these followers of Jesus. Whenever and wherever friends gathered to retell the stories, she was there, and she then retold them to her daughters and other neighbors. She loved learning more about Jesus, hearing about God, and building friendships with others. The stories carried her to the well and back each morning and sustained her through the daily task of feeding her family; and with the stories in her heart and friends at her side, the burdens felt lighter and the days more full of life.

Seventeen hundred and fifty years later, in a small thatched-roof cottage in a village an hour's ride from London, a man held his small journal closer to the lamp as he wrote his account of the evening's gathering. It had been a long day. He began working the fields before sunrise and labored alongside other men from the village until after sunset. But unlike many of the others, his day did not end with his work in the field. Instead, he washed up as best he could and ate a quick meal so that he could prepare his home, reread the Scripture quietly to himself, and pray for the Spirit's guidance. As Methodist Class Leader, he prayed for each person he expected to come before they arrived. One by one they began showing up until his home was filled with the welcome and laughter, the blessings and good-natured chatter of a dozen of his friends and brothers. Their congenial and affectionate greetings brought warmth beyond what his small hearth could provide. These men had also spent the day laboring, some in stables and fields and others in shops and kitchens.

When everyone had arrived, he reminded them of Mr. Wesley's rules for classes and about the covenant they had made with each other in order to belong: to attend the public worship of God, including the reading and expounding of the Holy Scriptures and receiving the Supper of the Lord, and to commit to private prayer and the searching of Scriptures. Leaning toward the lamp, he read to them of their pledge to watch over the souls of one another, to practice diligence and frugality, to do good in every way, and to be merciful as far as possible to all people. Then he led them in singing and prayer, and began to describe how he had experienced the week, joys and sorrows, temptations and trials, and times when God had delivered him. He asked the others about the state of their souls, and each in turn spoke of his life and God's grace during the week past. He shared the Scripture that he had prepared, and talked about the thoughts that had come to him about these verses while he had worked the fields during the day. He led them in praying for one another and then collected coins from each to give to the steward for the work of God, carefully recording the amount beside the name of each giver. He offered the blessing of Christ, and they bade him warm farewells to return to their own homes, leaving him with his journal. He noted attendance and marked his appraisal of the spiritual state of each member. Then he snuffed the lamp and took his rest. It had been a long day, but he felt grateful beyond words for his life, his faith, and his friends. He felt renewed, strengthened, and encouraged. By his work in the fields, he made a living. By this care of souls, he made a life.

Two hundred and fifty years later, a young woman pulls into the church parking lot just before the session begins. She's running a little late. Like most Tuesdays she's still wearing her suit from work, going through her evening a blur of movement from office to school to soccer practice to drive-thru to church. Her son dumps his fast-food wrappings in the trash bin beside the door as he carries his schoolbooks into the building. He'll work on homework while Mom does her "Bible thing." She slips into the room as the video begins. Her closest friend is there and welcomes her into the seat beside her. They had signed up for this together, deciding to "just do it" after years of wanting to study the Bible. The class also includes two couples; two older women; a graduate student from the university; and the leader, recently retired from the bank. She didn't know most of these people before they signed up for DISCIPLE Bible Study, but she's been amazed at how much she's learned from them as they've shared their thoughts about faith and God and Scripture and about how much she's come to care for them as they've shared their lives. The Tuesday evening study has become a time of refreshment for her each week, an oasis of encouragement, learning, and support. For ten minutes, they listen to a seminary professor on the video talk about the stories of Moses, his birth and marriage and encounter with God. Then they walk through the readings, sharing observations and questions.

Every day for the past week, she has spent time reading Scripture, sometimes lost in the archaic practices and customs and confused by the stories and characters. She has so many questions about God. She wasn't sure she had time for this kind of study, and sometimes even now she thinks she's wasting her time. Moses seems *way back then* and *way over there*. Then the leader talks about Moses' call—the bush, the fear and humility, and the excuses and justifications given to avoid doing what God asks. Her stomach tightens as she hears people tell about times they've felt called by God to do something and have repeated the same excuses themselves. She looks at her own notes from her reading through the week, and sees the questions she wrote. "How does God call people? Sometimes I feel called, but I've never heard voices or seen burning bushes. Am I being called?" She shares her questions with others and discovers that they wrestle with the same thoughts. The evening ends with prayer, and after she drives home with her son, sends him to bed, and nestles herself into her favorite chair, she finds herself praying, asking, and hoping, "What would you have *me* do, Lord?"

2.

Vibrant, fruitful, growing congregations practice Intentional Faith Development. From the first generation of Christians to the earliest Methodists to the youngest generations of faithful members today, the followers of Jesus mature in faith by learning together in community. Churches that practice Intentional Faith Development offer high quality learning experiences that help people understand Scripture, faith, and life in the supportive nurture of caring relationships. Sunday school classes, Bible studies, short-term topical studies, support groups that apply faith to particular life challenges, children's church, Vacation Bible School, United Methodist Women, camps, retreats, and youth fellowship groups are only a few of the countless ways by which churches help people probe God's will for their lives and for the world, and bring people together to strengthen the Body of Christ by building friendships and relationships. Christian disciples strive to develop faith and grow in Christ-likeness through study and learning, and God is best able to form disciples when people do this together and not by themselves.

Christ's gracious invitation through Radical Hospitality invites and welcomes us, and God's transforming presence in Passionate Worship opens our hearts to Christ's pardon, love, and grace, creating in us a desire to follow. Growing in Christ requires more than weekly worship though, and it is through Intentional Faith Development that God's Spirit works in us, perfecting us in the practice of love as we grow in the knowledge and love of God.

Learning in community replicates the way Jesus deliberately taught his disciples. His followers grew in their understanding of God and matured in their awareness of God's will for their lives as they listened to Jesus' stories, instructions, and lessons while gathering around dinner tables, on hillsides, and at the Temple. Jesus taught us to learn our faith this way.

Following the formation of the church by the Holy Spirit at Pentecost, the earliest communities of Christians thrived as "they devoted themselves to the apostles' teaching and fellowship, to the breaking of bread and the prayers" (Acts 2:42). Notice the dual reference to learning and community.

Paul sprinkles his instructions to the followers of Christ with encouragements to learn, grow, teach, and mature. He presents faith not as something static, a possession, or an all or nothing proposition, but rather as something we grow into and

> **"Bible Study Messes with Your Life!"**
>
> Carol joined a United Methodist Church, attended worship and Sunday school, and volunteered with various week-to-week projects and programs of the church. One turning point in Carol and her husband's faith journey was joining with a Volunteers-in-Mission work project overseas. Then she joined Disciple Bible Study. In the small, supportive community of her class, she encountered truths and insights she had been searching for. More than that, she found God calling her to radically change the direction and priorities of her life. She eventually offered herself to full-time Christian service, changed jobs, and now works as lay mission coordinator, focused on international ministries. "Bible study messes with your life!" is her good-humored but serious way of telling others about her faith journey. Learning in community helps people explore possibilities that God may have for them that they never would have considered on their own.

strive toward, a putting away of one's "former way of life, [the] old self" to clothe oneself "with the new self" (Ephesians 4:22, 24). We seek to have in us the mind that was in Christ Jesus, allowing God's Spirit to shape our thoughts, attitudes, values, and behaviors. Growing in Christ-likeness is the goal and end of the life of faith.

The change God works in us through the Spirit results in a deeper awareness of God's presence and will and an increasing desire to serve God and neighbor. By God's grace, we become new persons. "So if anyone is in Christ, there is a new creation: everything old has passed away; see, everything has become new!" (2 Corinthians 5:17)

This growth in Christ spans a lifetime. Paul writes, "Not that I have already obtained this or have already reached the goal; but I press on to make it my own, because Christ Jesus has made me his own . . . Straining forward to what lies ahead, I press on toward the goal" (Philippians 3:12-14). Faith moves, grows, changes, matures.

As we mature in Christ, God cultivates in us the fruit of the spirit: "love, joy, peace, patience, kindness, generosity, faithfulness, gentleness, and self-control" (Galatians 5:22-23). These are the qualities to which the Christian aspires; these are the qualities God's Spirit forms in us as we deepen our relationship with God through Christ.

These interior spiritual qualities are all radically relational, and we only learn them in the presence of others through the practice of love. They are honed in community, and not just by reading books and studying Scripture. They become real in our lives in the love we give and receive from others and in the things we learn and teach with others. Jesus said, "Where two or three are gathered in my name, I am there among them" (Matthew 18:20). Jesus taught in community so that we would learn to discover his presence in others.

The notion of growing in faith is central to Methodist practice. John Wesley taught of sanctification, the maturing in faith made possible by the Spirit as we grow in Christ-likeness. Wesley was concerned for Christian disciples beyond the initial stages of engagement with the church, and he wanted Methodists to go on from grace to grace, spending time in the presence of God's Word and God's people so that God's Spirit would create the heart anew. Opening ourselves to the sanctifying grace of God, we pray that by God's grace we are closer to Christ now than five years ago. And we pray that by the God's grace we will be closer to Christ and deeper in our relationship to God five years from now than we are today. Christian faith is not static but dynamic. It requires cultivation. Wesley was as passionate about Christians maturing toward the fullness of faith as he was about inviting Christians into the beginnings of faith. He called early Methodists to practices that fostered faith through learning in community, which results in the steady withering of the old nature while nurturing the fruits of the spirit. This steady maturing, full of setbacks, distractions, and missteps for sure, is the perfecting of the soul in love, growing in the image of God, fostering of an inner holiness. The end toward which we strive is having the same mind in us that was in Christ Jesus (Philippians 2:5).

The song "Day by Day" from the musical *Godspell* expresses the Christian disciple's desire to grow in the grace of Christ and to advance daily in the knowledge and love of God. In the musical, which is based upon the Gospel of Matthew, the cast acts out the parable of the unforgiving servant, in which a servant whose enormous debt was forgiven by his master refuses to forgive a much smaller debt owed to him by a fellow servant (Matthew 18:23-35). After Jesus explains that his followers must forgive each other from their hearts, the cast sings a beautiful prayer that asks God for three things: "To see thee more clearly, love thee more dearly, follow thee more nearly day by day" (*Godspell*, Stephen Schwartz, 1973).

As Wesley and the early Methodists realized, growth in faith does not come easily or automatically, but requires placing ourselves in community to learn the faith with others. Wesley commended the practices of public and family prayers, the searching of Scriptures, the receiving of Holy Communion, and the practice of works of mercy—all in supportive community. We learn the life of Christ and will of God by studying God's Word and through experience with other people of faith. The early Methodist Class meetings, like modern day DISCIPLE Bible Studies and effective Sunday school classes, provided the means to help people remain faithful in their journey toward Christ. By joining a Bible study or class, we place ourselves in the circumstances that are most advantageous for growth in faith. Bible study is not just about self-improvement but about setting ourselves where God can shape us, intentionally opening ourselves to God's Word and call. God uses faith-to-faith relationships to change us.

The practice of learning in community gives disciples a network of support, encouragement, and direction as we seek to grow in Christ. As we consciously appropriate the stories of faith with others, we discover that our questions, doubts, temptations, and missteps are not unusual but are part of the journey. We are emboldened to new ways of thinking about God and to new ways of exercising our faith in daily life. Others help us interpret God's Word for our lives, offering an antidote to inordinately self-referential or narcissistic interpretations that merely confirm our current lifestyles, attitudes, and behaviors. The fruit of the spirit that we see in Christ (Galatians 5:22-23) cannot be learned apart from a network of relationships. In the intimacy of small groups, we learn not only from writers and thinkers and people of the past through Scripture and books, but also from mentors and models and fellow travelers in our congregation. We give and receive the care of Christ by praying for one another, supporting one another through periods of grief and difficulty, and celebrating one another's joys and hopes. Sunday school classes, Bible studies, choirs, and other small groups are really little churches within the bigger church family, and they are the most likely places for us to learn to "rejoice with those who rejoice," and "weep with those who weep" (Romans 12:15). The sanctifying grace of God bears the human face of our fellow disciples.

And learning in community provides accountability for our faith journeys. A seminary professor used to say, "Everybody *wants to want* to study the Bible." He was referring to the contrast between our good intentions and our actual practices. How many people each year resolve to read the Bible, start with Genesis in January, and give up all hope of seeing their way through to the end by the time they reach Leviticus in February?

I'm a serious runner, and people often ask me how to get started on a running program. When I ask them what they've tried, they inevitably tell a story about New Year's resolutions and their enthusiastic jump out of bed when the alarm rings at six on the first morning. The eagerness lasts a few days, and during the second week when the alarm screams them awake at

---

"The Middle Doors"

The pastor and staff of a mid-sized congregation noticed that while the church received many new visitors, and a high percentage of them were joining the church, nevertheless attendance remained steady month after month. For several years the church had seen growth in attendance, and they couldn't figure out why it was leveling off now. The church practiced hospitality with excellence, with visitors and new members feeling welcomed at worship and into membership. But then after a few months, visitors and new members would drift away, become less consistent in attendance, and fall away altogether. To understand the situation better, the pastor visited with some members who had joined in the last several months.

six, they tell themselves, "There's nothing wrong with running at seven rather than six," and so they sleep another hour. By the third week, when the alarm rings at seven, they tell themselves, "There's no sense being fanatical about this; I don't have to run *every* day to be fit." And then the downward slide begins, from five times weekly to once a week, from two miles to one, from running to walking to nothing at all. That's the course of so many of our good intentions.

The answer in running, as well as in Bible study, is to covenant with friends who share the same interests and goals. If we know that people are waiting for us and expecting us at the park at six-thirty, then we'll roll out of bed at six even when we don't feel like it. In community there is a natural accountability. Covenanting together keeps us strong in our convictions and habits. That's why Jesus sent the disciples out two by two to go "to every town and place where he himself intended to go" (Luke 10:1). In pairs, the disciples could build each other up for the task; pray for one another; and support one another through the inevitable resist-

He discovered that people felt welcomed and supported when they first visited the church, and continued to feel a sense of belonging in worship. But when they tried to become part of Sunday school classes, men's organizations, choirs, and Bible studies, the groups felt cliquish and uninterested in welcoming new people. Even after some months of trying, they felt at the margins in these smaller groups and ministries. One woman said, "Before I moved here, I was the kitchen chief in my old church for years. I didn't expect to do that again here, but I hoped to join the cooking team. When I showed up to help with a dinner, they handed me napkins and told me to put them on the tables, and then I just stood around by myself the rest of the evening. I felt like they didn't need me or want me."

The pastor and staff soon realized that "the front door" was working well as people felt invited and welcomed. But they were slipping out "the back door" because they were discovering too many of "the middle doors" were closed tight.

They began a series of teaching events and lessons in the adult classes, mission teams, service organizations, choirs, and Bible studies to try to move the culture of hospitality deeper into the life of the church. After some months, they noticed that the small groups began to grow, and with them the worship attendance began to trend up again. Most new members will not feel like they really belong to the church until they find meaningful connections in small groups beyond the worship experience. Are your church's "middle doors" open?

67

ances, difficulties, misjudgments, and false starts. We learn in community because others keep us faithful to the task of growth in Christ. That's why John Wesley organized the early Methodists into classes, bands, and societies, and that's why churches offer Sunday school classes and Bible studies and small group ministries. The practices of faith are too demanding without support from others. Other Christians help us pray, read Scripture, exercise love and forgiveness, and explore and respond to the will of God for our lives.

Dietrich Bonheoffer reminds us that an incomparable joy results from the physical presence of other Christians. We see "in the companionship of a fellow Christian a physical sign of the gracious presence of Christ." In community, the Christian no longer seeks "his justification in himself, but in Jesus Christ alone." According to Bonhoeffer, every Christian needs another Christian when she or he becomes uncertain and discouraged. The Christ in one's own heart is weaker than the Christ in the word of a brother or sister (*Life Together*, Harper & Row, 1954, p. 20).

This all underscores the importance of faith development. Why add the adjective *intentional* to describe the practice for churches that are vibrant, fruitful, growing congregations? *Intentional* refers to deliberate effort, purposeful action toward an end, and high prioritization. It highlights the significance of faith development and contrasts those congregations that take it seriously with those that offer it haphazardly and inconsistently, without new initiative, plan, or purpose.

Intentional Faith Development describes the practice of churches that view the ministries of Christian education and formation, small group work, and Bible study as absolutely critical to their mission and that consistently offer opportunities for people of all ages, interests, and faith experiences to learn in community. They consciously and deliberately cover the whole age spectrum, fostering faith development outside of worship during the course of the year for children, youth, young adults, singles, couples, middle-aged adults, and older adults. They support and maintain existing Sunday school classes, studies, choirs, and women's and men's organizations, but they also continually fill the gaps with short-term, long-term, and topical small group ministries and start new classes especially designed for visitors and new members. Churches that practice Intentional Faith Development know the secret of small groups and constantly offer new possibilities for people to engage Christ by engaging one another.

3.

The pastor of a small, open country congregation wrestled with how best to provide opportunities for Bible study and fellowship for members who have busy family schedules and live miles from the church and from one another. Attempts to host weekday evening studies at the church brought together the same few long-time members who always attended faithfully. The pastor supported these efforts but particularly wanted to reach some of the younger families who didn't participate as fully in such ministries. One day she shared her dilemma and desire with one of the younger families and casually asked whether the family would consider hosting an hour-and-a-half study every other week in their home if she could get a few other families to attend. The family enthusiastically agreed, and a few weeks later they had their first home Bible study on a Tuesday night in the host's living room with three other families present. The pastor led an easy-going discussion with the adults and teens about a chapter of Scripture, occasionally provoking animated conversation about Jesus and his parables, and then led them in prayer together. The younger children played together in a back room. This worked so well that the pastor felt emboldened to ask another family on the other side of the county for the same favor of hosting a few others for Bible study. They graciously agreed. The pastor now leads two groups on alternate Tuesday evenings that reach about seven couples and families. Both groups then wanted to gather once every few months as a larger gathering to share dinner, Bible study, and prayers. Delight and joy energizes the conversations, and the families look forward with eagerness to their times together.

The pastor learned several lessons from her experience. First, people desire fellowship and want to learn about the faith, but they have trouble squeezing it into their lives. The more the church can do to accommodate, the better. Second, if congregations keep the end in mind (offering quality learning in community), their leaders may have to break out of usual patterns and expectations of place, frequency, and curriculum to reach people. What about the extra work of leading two studies away from the church? She answers, "What pastor wouldn't give an evening a week to teach the faith to more than 20 percent of her worshiping congregation? This is huge for us, and I only hope we can do more in the future!"

A larger church tried unsuccessfully several times to launch a new young adult Sunday school class. Church leaders had the tactics down right: they'd develop a list of sixty to eighty names of members, visitors, and friends between the ages of nineteen and twenty-eight; they'd recruit a couple of young adults to lead and teach the class; and after much publicity, correspondence, and phone invitations, they'd host an evening dinner party before the launch of the Sunday morning class. This had worked for starting new classes for other ages just fine. About twenty young adults would attend the dinner, and about fifteen would come to the first few weeks of classes, but after three months the class would inevitably dwindle to four or five people and then die out. The church repeated this pattern every twelve to eighteen months for several years. They were stumped on how to get good quality teaching and fellowship going for young adults.

As they prepared for their next attempt, a married couple in their mid-fifties stepped forward to offer their help. These "empty-nesters" had children of their own who were young adults, and they seemed unlikely candidates for teaching the class. But they were mature in their own faith, had taught many classes before, and had an inviting and accepting graciousness as they worked with people. They felt God had nudged them toward this ministry, they genuinely loved young adults, and they promised to give the work their best time and energy. The pastor, staff, and nurture team approved their leadership, and the couple set to work. They contacted young adults one by one and couple by couple to talk about their hopes for the class. They checked websites, made phone calls to other churches, and visited with other leaders of successful programs for young adults to get more ideas. They discovered that lumping college students with young couples starting families was not going to work, and they chose to focus on young couples. After weeks of personal conversations, they formed a small group to discuss plans and preferences for how to proceed. Most of the couples with young children wanted to bring their children to the opening dinner. (This pattern of preferring to include their children in as many events as possible continued for years.) The first gathering had fifty to sixty people, and the leaders described the purpose of the class, the topics they would begin with, and some of the other activities and ministries they might do together. From the beginning, the class began to demonstrate extraordinary care for one another, especially when couples gave birth or faced illness among their children. The young adults adopted an invitational stance, always searching to bring others in. Within a few months, they were looking for service projects that could use the talents and passions of the members. The class launched successfully, maintained strong attendance that continued to grow, developed an outward focus, and continues to serve large numbers of young adults today.

Meanwhile, the church staff considered alternatives for the college-aged young adults. Early morning Sunday school classes were not attracting the college crowd. The youth director met for lunch with several college students to talk about their interests and the rhythms of college life. Late Sunday evenings, college students returned to the campus area and wanted to see each other to catch up on the weekend's activities. They always stayed up late anyway and were usually scrounging for something to eat after weekends of work or play. So the youth director invited all the college students to her home at nine o'clock on Sunday evening, and the students spent a couple of hours together eating, catching up, talking about questions of faith, and praying. Sunday evening allowed students to reconnect with each other after the weekend and gave them a chance to spiritually prepare for the challenges of the week to come. They decided to meet every other Sunday night at nine.

What did the pastors and staff learn through these experiences? First, keep trying. Don't give up. Try different times, places, leaders, and formats, but keep trying. Second, the secret is relationships, relationships, relationships. Young people want to be treated with respect. They want to feel valued, and they hunger for a sense of belonging. Like all adults, they want to determine their own direction and be given responsibilities equal to their gifts. Third, beware of lumping young adults into a single category when there are significant differences between singles, couples, couples with children, college students, and non-college working young adults. Fourth, the successful leadership by the couple in their fifties helped the church staff see something they had missed before. Many young adults feel estranged from their own parents, often because of divorce, remarriage, or other conflict while they were growing up, and they want to relate to couples in their parents' generation who treat them as adults and who can model a maturing faith, a solid marriage, and the successful navigation of parenting's rough waters. They're searching for faith mentors and models. Fifth, young adults may not have much experience in matters of faith and may feel self-conscious about their lack of knowledge, but they nevertheless hunger for relationship, for faith, and for opportunities to make a positive difference in the lives of others. They are suspicious of the forms of religion but are attracted by the practices of prayer, learning, and serving. Finally, no small groups survive for long without the support, leadership, and help of the laity. Nor do they survive without the active support, encouragement, and permission of the pastor.

The practice of Intentional Faith Development takes a thousand forms. Some churches offer pre-packaged, high commitment learning experiences, such as DISCIPLE Bible Study, *Companions in Christ, Beginnings, Alpha,* the United Methodist *Treasures of the Transformed Life* (forty-day church-wide study), Rick Warren's *Forty Days of Purpose,* or *Bible Study Fellowship.* Others rely heavily on retreats, such as *The Walk to Emmaus, Chrysalis,* marriage enrichment weekends, or mini-retreats that they plan and resource themselves. Others overlay small group work with ministry and mission and train people as Stephen Ministers, pastoral care teams, visitation teams, choirs, praise bands, prayer circles, or Volunteers in Mission teams. Others deepen the quality of fellowship and learning in traditional settings such as adult Sunday school classes or United Methodist Women's and United Methodist Men's organizations. Others emphasize support groups that address critical needs such as Alcoholics Anonymous, divorce recovery workshops, grief support groups, or Alzheimer's family support organizations. And countless churches simply create their own setting, title, and focus, offering short-term or long-term learning academies, Lenten studies, Advent retreats, or topical studies on the Bible or on books about social or faith issues. Even small churches can offer robust ministries of learning, growing, and maturing in faith by creating new opportunities for long-term members and newcomers to learn in community. It only takes "two or three gathered in [Jesus'] name" to experience the presence of Christ and to grow together in faith.

At one church I served, we offered DISCIPLE Bible Study within the first few months after I arrived as pastor. Interest was so high that thirty-seven people signed up, and I was the only trained teacher available. We divided people into groups that met on different nights and began the study. At first I felt overwhelmed, but after some months I realized the extraordinary value of leading in-depth Bible study with so many key leaders and members of the church. I came to know them, and they got to know their new pastor. The study afforded us the opportunity to discuss topics (such as tithing, ministry to the poor, and the purpose of the church) that would have taken years to develop by other means. The following year, we had more teachers and offered more classes until eventually more than two hundred members had taken DISCIPLE Bible Study.

DISCIPLE Bible Study changes peoples' lives. In the church I served, people discerned their call to differing forms of lay ministry within the church, and a few went on to full-time Christian service. The practice of tithing increased, worship attendance became more consistent, and members developed a deeper appreciation for the sacraments. For the next ten years, virtually all significant lay leadership for new children's programs, mission initiatives, Sunday school classes, worship services, and stewardship emphases came from those members who had deepened their understanding of the faith through DISCIPLE Bible Study. The fundamental changes in faith and habit brought by Christ persist and become fruitful only when sustained by continual learning in community.

Bible study changes churches. When church leaders take their own spiritual growth seriously and immerse themselves in the study of Scripture, in prayer, and in fellowship, they understand the purpose of the church and the point of ministry differently. Peter Drucker has said that "the purpose of leadership in the church is not to make the church more business-like, but to make the church more church-like." While church leaders should apply their knowledge of business, accounting, real estate, the law, and banking to enhance the church's effectiveness and accountability, they cannot lose sight of the purpose of the church, which is derived from the life, teaching, ministry, death, and resurrection of Jesus Christ. How can church leaders make good faith decisions for the congregation without proper grounding in the faith? The decision on whether or not the church should make its facilities available to Alcoholics Anonymous cannot be reduced to lease contracts; it's a ministry decision. Whether the church should build a new youth center, fund an overseas mission trip, or support a local soup kitchen is a decision not reducible to a mere cost-benefit analysis. These decisions require hearts of faith that explore the will of God as well as minds that review the financial reports. Vibrant, fruitful, growing churches are led by lay people and pastors who intentionally work to grow in the grace of Jesus Christ and in the knowledge and love of God and who understand the need for intimate Christian fellowship and intentional instruction in the faith.

4.

Churches that practice Intentional Faith Development not only offer high quality traditional adult Sunday school classes for learning and fellowship, they also initiate and support weekday evening studies, home groups, "Brown Bag" lunch Bible studies, and a host of opportunities for faith studies at varying times and places to make them as accessible and convenient as possible. They focus on the schedules and interests of the people they seek to serve, even if it doesn't fit the usual weekly church schedule. They're not afraid of trying youth meetings or college groups at odd times and in unexpected places if that's what works better for students than Sunday morning. They offer study and learning groups that involve varying levels of commitment and experience so that everyone can plug in somewhere, with some studies requiring no preparation at all and others requiring in-depth reading. They offer short-term classes and long-term studies as well as ongoing opportunities that people can attend at any time. They seek to have so many people in small group ministries that the total participants in all classes, choirs, and teams exceeds 50 percent of their weekly worship attendance.

Congregations that practice Intentional Faith Development not only provide new and varied small group ministries of learning and fellowship for their long-term members, but they also start new groups particularly adapted to the needs of new members, visitors, and people not yet attending the church. They realize the power of special topics and interests to attract unchurched people, and they advertise and invite beyond the walls of their own church. Such churches realize that the most accessible small groups to new people are new groups, and so they constantly try to initiate, invite, and support new opportunities for learning in community to help assimilate people into the life of the church.

Pastors and staff members of churches that value Intentional Faith Development not only publicly support and help lead Bible studies and classes, they also highlight the importance of continuing faith development in sermons, lessons, and newsletter articles. With Wesley, they express as much concern for their members growing in the fullness of faith as in crossing the threshold at the beginnings of faith. Even when the language of sanctification is not explicitly used, themes of maturing in faith recur in the core values of the congregation. The notion of growing in faith by learning in community becomes widely known, highly valued, and broadly practiced. Pastors, staff, and lay leaders continually invite and encourage newcomers in worship to take the next step toward congregational engagement by becoming part of a small group study, class, or work team.

Congregations that take seriously the practice of Intentional Faith Development explore ways of forming learning communities using new technologies. They initiate blogs (web logs), chat rooms, and Listservs,

74

and they experiment with e-mail Bible studies for particular niches of people or around special topics. Many people prefer to read Scripture and "talk" with others over the internet, giving them time to think about things before they respond, and extending conversations throughout the week. Churches also make sermons, special lessons, and presentations downloadable so that members, friends, and guests can listen on their own time while driving, running, or working out.

Churches that practice Intentional Faith Development not only form faith through educational affiliation groups such as Bible studies and Sunday school classes but also understand and support the powerful impact that task oriented small groups (such as choirs, praise bands, Stephen Ministers, cooking crews, and mission teams) have on forming faith. They help these groups understand their significance for faith formation and develop a culture of hospitality to welcome new people, and they see to it that such ministries are laced with prayer and characterized by mutual care and support of its members.

In churches that intentionally strengthen their small group ministries, pastors and church leaders work toward the objective that every learning group has fellowship components and every fellowship ministry has elements and practices that lead to faith formation. They encourage Sunday school classes and Bible studies to have fellowship dinners, Christmas parties, service projects, prayer support, and other practices that deepen community. In a parallel way, they encourage groups that are formed around common interests and simple fellowship (such as aerobics classes, parenting classes, book clubs, senior adult travel groups, and financial planning workshops) to include elements of prayer, devotionals, and invitations to other ministries of the church.

Congregations that practice Intentional Faith Development are not afraid of failure and willingly initiate new ministries of learning in community, knowing that some will take root and last for generations and others will continue only a few months and then fade away. They realize God is able to change lives by working through our imperfect attempts to start new Sunday school classes or fellowship groups, even when they last only a few months. In starting new groups, they don't allow those who have no interest in the topic, time, or setting to veto those who are interested and willing, and so they're not afraid to start groups with low numbers, trusting that God will make use of the time to help those who attend.

Congregations that excel at Intentional Faith Development rely not only on their pastors to lead teaching and formation ministries, but they also invite, support, and train lay people to lead small groups, teach Bible studies, and coordinate support groups. They take seriously the care and nurture of teachers, volunteers, and other lay coordinators, supporting them with appreciation, resources, and training. They lift up teachers and leaders in prayer, recognize them in worship through consecration or appreciation services, and send personal notes of encouragement. They develop systems to see that the leaders' needs are provided for so that no leader of small groups feels alone, unequipped, or unappreciated. For more formal programs, such as Disciple Bible Study or Stephen Ministries, congregational leaders readily support formal training by paying costs for required workshops and seminars.

Churches shaped by Intentional Faith Development not only rely upon on-site, at-the-church settings for formation events, but also know the value of taking people away from their daily lives for one to three day retreats to focus on matters of faith and life. They develop overnight retreats for women, men, couples, youth, and families. Purposes for such periods of time away together range widely, from Advent and Lenten retreats to topical events with guest speakers. They often use books and special resources and include times of learning, reflection, fellowship, sharing, worship, and quiet.

For churches aspiring to Intentional Faith Development, not only the laity but also the pastor and staff are expected to practice learning in community. Pastors and staff actively work to deepen their own faith and not just enhance their skills for ministry. Pastors study Scripture not only for sermons and to prepare for teaching but also to deepen their own relationship with God. They participate in forms of community with other pastors or laypersons. Such communities may include lectionary study groups, covenant groups, support groups, or learning networks. Lay people sense that their pastor is growing, learning, and deepening in faith.

Churches that practice Intentional Faith Development form affiliation groups not only around Bible studies and explicit topics of faith but also around common interests, experiences, and challenges, such as grief or divorce recovery, substance abuse, parenting, cancer survivors, managing debt, financial planning, and middle-aged adults dealing with aging parents. Topics that bring together people with compelling life challenges are endless. Sometimes faith plays a central role in these conversations, yet other times faith figures into discussions in a less explicit way as people struggle with significant issues in the supportive environment of the church. Churches display a willingness and eagerness to make their facilities available to reasonable requests of support organizations whose purposes are consistent with the church's mission.

Churches that practice Intentional Faith Development know that maturation in Christ is always about content *and* relationship. Ideas change people, and people change people; and God uses both together to work on our behalf and to shape our lives in the image of Christ. Transformation comes through learning in community.

Congregational leaders that practice Intentional Faith Development carefully con-

---

"Meals for New Moms"

Adjusting to the addition of a new baby in the family isn't easy, and many new mothers and fathers find themselves falling into a pattern of ordering pizza, bringing home fast food, and otherwise "making do" during the first few hectic, exhausting days after returning from the hospital with a newborn. One church decided to help out with a "Meals for New Moms" ministry. Members of the church prepare homemade dinners and deliver them to the house of new parents several times during the first couple of weeks after coming home. New moms are often moved to tears by the thoughtfulness, helpfulness, and care during this important family time. This caring and supportive ministry models love and exemplifies grace and teaches young families about serving, caring, and helping. Learning to care for one another in community develops faith for the givers and receivers of this thoughtful ministry.

---

sider the full life cycle of members and look for ways the church forms faith at every stage. They look for gaps and opportunities and unmet needs to round out their ministries. They inventory their complete annual program of ministry for elementary age children: Sunday school, children's choir, mid-week programs, Vacation Bible School, Christmas programs, children's church, children's mission project, and all other ways they touch the lives of children during the year. They ask themselves if their ministry is sufficient, full, helpful, and effective. They ask how they can do better. In similar fashion, they consider preschool children, youth, college students, young adults, singles, couples, middle-aged adults, and seniors. They honestly assess how they are doing in providing programs and small groups to sustain growth in the faith for people at every stage of life. Rather than providing haphazard, hit-and-miss, eclectic education and formation ministries, they seek to cultivate growth in faith in more intentional ways that address unmet needs and invite more and more people into formative relationships, habits, and practices that help people grow in the knowledge and love of God.

5.

The gracious welcome of Christ deepens our sense of belonging through the congregation's practice of Radical Hospitality. God turns our hearts and minds toward Christ through Passionate Worship, gracing us with the desire to follow Christ more nearly. The practice of Intentional Faith Development matures our understanding and experience of Christ. No matter how dedicated our efforts, the transformation of human hearts and minds is God's work through the Holy Spirit, and intentionally learning in community is our way of placing ourselves in the hands of God so that God can sculpt our souls and recreate us in the image of Christ. The refreshing intimacy and companionship of fellow Christians learning together engrafts us onto the Body of Christ and becomes a means of grace by which God awakens a heightened desire to love our neighbors. Interior spiritual renewal and growth changes outward behaviors as following Christ becomes a way of life. The growing desire to serve Christ by loving our neighbor creates an eagerness to respond to the call of God to works of mercy, compassion, and justice. This leads us to the next practice of vibrant, fruitful, growing congregations, the practice of Risk-Taking Mission and Service.

Conversation Questions:

- List all the weekly small group ministries and activities of your church that occur outside of worship as a means of helping people to study, learn, experience, and practice the faith. How is faith nurtured for children? Youth? Young adults? Singles? Couples? Middle-aged and older adults? How are the needs of those who are new to the church addressed?
- How does your congregation start new groups, studies, or classes? How are newcomers, visitors, and those outside of the church invited to new studies or short-term classes? Does the number of participants in small group ministries total at least 50 percent of worship attendance for the congregation?

Group Activity:

In groups of two or three, outline a year's worth of learning opportunities that you would like to attend if they were offered. What do you most want to learn about the faith, and what are the settings that are most favorable to you for learning?

Share with your group one learning experience in your faith life that has changed how you live in a significant way. How did you learn it, and with whom? How have you shared it with others?

CHAPTER FOUR

THE PRACTICE OF RISK-TAKING MISSION AND SERVICE

"Truly I tell you, just as you did it to one of the least of these who are members of my family, you did it to me." (Matthew 25:40)

1.

Our hosts greeted us at the airport, and after some minutes of squeezing luggage into tight spaces and cramping people into van seats, we set off away from the city into valleys green with tropical forests. The winding narrow road rose and fell, and with every quick turn, we'd all lean heavily into each other. With each bump and dip, we'd gasp and groan and joke and hold on even tighter. Daylight faded as we felt the smooth pavement give way to gravelly roadbed and eventually to heavily pitted dry dirt. Street lights and car headlamps became fewer and fewer until we were maneuvering slowly around and up and down giant potholes in total darkness, our high beams providing the only illumination in sight. Our van drew to a stop alongside a fence in what appeared to be an unpaved village street, and when our driver turned off the headlights, the black of the moonless night swallowed us up. We could not see anything, but we could hear voices of people, lots of people, crowding against the van. When we stepped out, we could feel the press of people young and old, shaking hands, offering to carry our packs and supplies, welcoming us, and blessing us. We shuffled up steps and through a gate to a small parsonage where a lantern lit a crowded kitchen. Every room seemed packed with people wanting to help. We learned that the generator that usually provides several evening hours of light had failed, a misunderstanding about dates and times meant the meal was not ready, and a miscommunication about numbers resulted in fewer cots and rooms than there were people on our team. Gradually, team members stepped forth from dark corners of the room, volunteering to sleep in chairs or to use sleeping bags on the floor. Our host briefly reminded us of various risks associated with latrines, malaria, and well-water. The burning enthusiasm that carried the team through the early morning flight many hours earlier seemed to flicker low, and in the gentle light cast by the lantern, you could see people mulling over our situation, and you could almost hear them thinking, "What in the world are we doing here?" Late in the night, food arrived, and after a quiet gathering for devotions and prayers, we found our rest, wondering what the morning would bring.

Roosters crowed us awake before the early tropical sun, and we could hear the voices of the neighborhood around us, women pat-patting tortillas for breakfast and men sharpening machetes before heading to the fields. We stepped out on the porch to see a procession of young girls with bowls on their heads and coins in their hands, taking the morning march to the mill to buy *masa* for their families. The smell of burning wood filled the streets as people set to work preparing food, cleaning clothes, and taking hand baths from basins beside their homes. In a village without electricity or a sewage system, with no cars and only the occasional bus, neighbors drew water from common faucets, shared bicycles, and walked together in small clusters to faraway markets. Our hosts welcomed us with breakfast, and soon we gathered to hear the details of our work assignment, which was laying floor tiles for the village Methodist Church. For the next five days, from early morning until late evening, we mixed concrete side-by-side with local teens, laid tiles under the supervision of local craftsmen (who sometimes visibly cringed at our amateur efforts!), and shared meals with the pastor and the church members. Some of our team taught and learned songs with the children, told Bible stories, and helped with artwork. We offered a come-as-you-are-whenever-you-want Vacation Bible School for all ages of children, teens, and parents. We worshiped with our host congregation under the stars, preaching, praying, and singing in English and Spanish, amazed at how lively and moving worship can be without buildings, air conditioning, sound systems, pianos, hymnals, bulletins, a wall clock, or even a common language! They sang for us in Spanish, and we sang for them in English; their pastor preached in Spanish, offering greetings in English while our pastor stammered with his imperfect Spanish to offer greetings in return. Five days later and after flurries of work deep into Saturday night, the sanctuary was complete for Sunday morning, and we watched with delight and humility as young children danced barefoot along the fresh, cool tiles while members of the congregation lifted their voices in prayer and song. The next day ended our mission experience all too soon. We packed our luggage, and with genuine affection and mutual thankfulness for the time together, we prayed with our hosts and then squeezed into the vans for the ride back to the airport.

I've just described a United Methodist Volunteers in Mission work project to Honduras, taken by a team of college students and retirees, dentists and teachers, musicians and bankers. Alter a few details, and this might describe a thousand different projects church teams complete each year in Central and South America, Eastern Europe, Asia, Africa, or in areas of the United States marked by special need or touched by natural disaster.

I'm acutely aware of the risks of projects that bring together two or more distinct cultures with the attendant inequities of wealth and power and differences in value, practice, custom, dress, and lifestyle. Sometimes paternalistic and patronizing attitudes spoil good intentioned efforts; assumptions of cultural supremacy poison honest learning; and insensitive words, dominating personalities; and self-righteous attitudes make some cultural interchanges about as appealing as grating fingernails the length of a dry chalkboard. And such projects are seldom the most cost efficient way to achieve concrete results. Sending funds without people would

---

"Interweaving Cultures"

One United Methodist congregation had worked on service projects in Mexico for years, cooperating with the autonomous Methodist Church in that country, building houses and renovating churches. After hurricane Katrina devastated New Orleans, the U.S. congregation felt called to prepare a team to help clean and rebuild. A pastor and congregation from Mexico also wanted to help. Together the two congregations, one from Texas and the other from Mexico, planned a work project comprised of volunteers from both countries. The joint work team coordinated with a Louisiana church, sleeping on floors, working clean up and repair during the days, and offering prayers and worship for local church members. The intermingling of three cultures bore witness to the Spirit's ability to weave and strengthen life even during the most difficult of challenges.

have gotten the floor laid with less cost, at the sacrifice of the intercultural, interpersonal learnings and connections.

On the other hand, such projects done well and with the proper spirit absolutely change lives. Teams of volunteers build homes, construct churches, repair parsonages, erect wheelchair ramps, establish clinics, dispense medical care, paint schools, dig wells, widen roads, and teach children. The best of them don't focus on the materials and buildings so much as on the relationships and people, and these projects usually achieve a level of genuine engagement, of mutual listening and learning.

Mission initiatives change the lives of those who receive the help. One woman who lost nearly every earthly possession in a flood said, "I didn't cry when the water destroyed my home. But when I saw people from the church traveling from so far away to help me clean up and rebuild, I couldn't stop crying." Nothing is as hard as a lonely struggle, and discovering that others care enough to help, to give their time and work, and to sacrifice on another's behalf is a touch of grace. The work that teams complete changes lives. A cinderblock house with a concrete floor replaces houses of patchwork boards with no floor at all, vaccinations and antibiotics prevent suffering, newly dug wells save miles of hard daily walking by hundreds, ramps and wheelchairs give people access to their communities as they come and go from home more easily. Never underestimate the transforming power of small actions. God uses caring and effective volunteer work to change the lives and conditions of people across the world.

Hands-on mission projects change the lives of volunteers. Nobody returns from such service and looks at his or her own life in the same way. Intercultural experiences and genuine engagement with the poor have the effect of shining a light back on one's own culture, and extravagance, consumerism, materialism, and waste of abundance are seen in new ways. Countless pastors have discerned their call to ministry through active engagement with people on service projects. Retired people have returned and rededicated their life work after Volunteers In Mission (VIM) projects, and college students have changed careers because of the impact of face-to-face, hand-in-hand mission work in a culture other than their own. Recently, I wore a t-shirt with an "Iglesia Metodista de Honduras" logo as I stepped into a mobile phone store to seek repairs. The young man working on my phone looked up, saw the shirt, paused, and lifted his eyes as if he were looking a thousand miles away, saying, "I've been to Honduras. On a work team with my church. It changed my life." Then he looked back down at the phone and continued his work. God uses mission projects to mature and form disciples and to prepare them for greater service.

Mission initiatives change churches. Even when a small percentage of the membership immerse themselves in significant mission and service, the texture of church life changes, and the language of service and outreach begins to form conversations and priorities. Ministries of mercy and justice begin to take root. Tolerance increases; youth programs evolve beyond parties, videos, beach trips and amusement parks; and these ministries become focused on changing lives and making a difference for the purposes of Christ. The interweaving of lives across culture, class, color, and age boundaries genuinely enriches the congregation and makes Scripture stories come alive in real experience. God strengthens the Body of Christ through mission and service, and God empowers the Body of Christ through witness.

2.

Vibrant, fruitful, growing congregations practice Risk-Taking Mission and Service. Risk-Taking Mission and Service includes the projects, the efforts, and work people do to make a positive difference in the lives of others for the purposes of Christ, whether or not they will ever be part of the community of faith. Some churches practice Risk-Taking Mission and Service by sending work teams to Mozambique, Russia, Mexico, or Honduras, or they assist closer to home in clean up and reconstruction after hurricanes or tornadoes. Other churches focus on projects within their own community, such as after-school programs for at-risk children, food banks and soup kitchens, and ministries of witness aimed at forming public policy. Others get involved in ministries to senior adults in retirement centers, regular services for the incarcerated, and efforts to challenge and change unjust or inhumane systems that affect the poor.

Risk-Taking Mission and Service is one of the fundamental activities of church life that is so critical that failure to practice it in some form results in a deterioration of the church's vitality and ability to make disciples of Jesus Christ. When churches turn inward, using all resources for their own survival and caring only for their own people, then spiritual vitality wanes. By offering the Radical Hospitality of Christ, church members bring others into contact with the church, and through Passionate Worship, God transforms them. People grow in faith and love through Intentional Faith Development, and God's process of forming disciples continues as people practice Christ's compassion with their neighbors through Risk-Taking Mission and Service.

"It's Not Just About Roofs and Floors"

A predominantly Anglo congregation held an annual three-day home repair and construction project in poorer neighborhoods to build wheelchair ramps, replace roofs, and redo plumbing and flooring for people who did not have the resources for such things. The work focused on a predominantly Hispanic neighborhood, and for three days the targeted homes turned into work sites with dozens of volunteers arriving in SUVs, holding their Starbuck's cups, unloading high-cost tools, talking on cell phones, and playing music while they worked. Team members noticed that the family they were serving retreated more from the site and the workers each day. They became concerned about how the people who lived in the homes felt about this experience.

This motivated the planners to solicit Hispanic sociology students from a nearby university and contract with them to do a follow up visit to each of the families they had worked with over the past several years. The students compiled an assessment tool to evaluate what the experience had been like for the families to receive work teams in their neighborhood. They conducted their surveys in Spanish without church members present. Families reported feeling a loss of control about their homes, self-consciousness and embarrassment before their neighbors about receiving help from so many people, rejection at their efforts to assist in the repairs, and awkwardness about language limitations. They appreciated the work done on their homes, but they often felt invisible as people talked about them in front of them. Based on

Ordinary Christian service takes many forms. Keeping the church alive and fulfilling its purpose require the active and regular service of members and visitors. The volunteer impulse, animated by the spirit of God in Christ, causes people to give time generously to help with ushering or parking, assist in the kitchen, sing in the choir, serve on church boards and planning committees, visit home bound or hospitalized members, teach Sunday school, transport youth, take gifts and literature to first-time visitors, and/or help with the clean up team around the church. Such basic and ordinary service is the lifeblood that gives the congregation strength. The phrase "to equip the saints for the work of ministry" (Ephesians 4:12) means that churches invite, encourage, prepare, and cultivate such ordinary service so the ministry of Christ thrives. The operations and ministry of a congregation require the cooperative and helpful spirit of those who love the church and want to see it run smoothly and effectively to fulfill its mission, and the fruit of their service includes tasks well-done, community formation, connection to one another, learning the meaning of church, and changed lives for those within and beyond the congregation. A church without generous and willing service by its members can never practice Radical Hospitality, Passionate Worship, Intentional Faith Development, or Extravagant Generosity since these depend upon the leadership, time, effort, prayers, sweat, and tears of members and friends of the church. Basic service builds the Body of

these responses, church leaders radically revamped the program with far greater sensitivity and respect for the families they serve, more intentional engagement, and mutual conversation in the residents' native language throughout the project. Even the best-intentioned projects can benefit from the analysis, "How can we do better? How do we build goodwill and positive relationships as well as buildings?"

Christ, and the responsibility falls to all who love the church to use their talents and energy. Making ourselves useful for the purpose of building the Body of Christ imbues our lives with purpose and connects us to others. Genuine and generous service makes a difference.

The word *mission* turns church service outward. Mission reminds congregations that Christ's compassion, grace, mercy, and love extend to the entire world, and these fruits are cultivated not only within the walls of the church or among the people of the Body of Christ who are regularly seen and already known. Mission refers to the positive difference made in the lives of people beyond the inner circle of the church. Mission spreads the faith by exemplifying the compassion, mercy, and justice of Christ in the world. For many churches, such work involves outreach in their communities as they establish food pantries to serve the homeless, sponsor scouting programs in underserved areas, advocate for fair housing practices, gather coats for the Salvation Army, collect toys for Toys for Tots, and provide formula for babies in need. Mission also involves the focus on work abroad, supporting clinics, schools, or partner congregations in other parts of the world through financial or other donations. Nearly every congregation supports or offers some level of mission, relying upon the volunteer help and financial generosity of members, Sunday school classes, women's organizations, or mission committees.

Service, offering oneself in the deliberate effort to improve the conditions of others, is rooted in more than three thousand years of faith tradition. Nothing is more central to faith identity and to the church's mission than transforming the lives and conditions of people by offering oneself in God's name. Nearly every page of Scripture shows people serving God by serving others.

The earliest written Scriptures record a consistent emphasis upon justice, compassion, respect, and love for the neighbor. The books of law not only restrain violence, fraud, theft, and harm but call us to "love [our] neighbor as [ourself]" (Leviticus 19:18). Scripture inextricably links love of God to love of neighbor and calls people to charity, justice, and mercy. The Psalms reveal the nature and intent of God in passages replete with reminders that God is the "lover of justice" (Psalm 99:4); that God "loves righteousness and justice" (Psalm 33:5); that the people of God are "to do justice for the orphan and the oppressed (Psalm 10:18); and to "give justice to the weak and the orphan" (Psalm 82:3). The theme continues in the writings of the prophets, "He has told you, O mortal, what is good; and what does the LORD require of you, but to do justice, and to love kindness; and to walk humbly with your God" (Micah 6:8).

Jesus echoes the words of the prophets to describe his purpose: "The Spirit of the Lord is upon me, because he has anointed me to bring good news to the poor. He has sent me to proclaim release to the captives and recovery of sight to the blind, to let the oppressed go free, to proclaim the year of the Lord's favor" (Luke 4:18-19). The stories, teachings, and parables of Jesus consistently point toward God's love for the poor, the sick, the outcast, and those most vulnerable to the oppressions of society. Against the resistance of the religious elite and contrary to the advice of his disciples, Jesus lifts up the bent-over woman on the Sabbath, touches the unclean with healing power, releases the paralyzed from his bed, eats with tax-collectors in their homes, and risks the violence of the mob to intervene for the woman caught in adultery. In teaching and action, he shows that God's way includes costly demonstrations of unexpected love to the least likely. The stories of the good Samaritan, the father risking humiliation to welcome back his prodigal son, and the rich person neglecting Lazarus at his own doorstep all consistently show who Jesus is; and through Jesus, we see what God intends for us.

Jesus tells that in every act of compassion, people touch Christ. "I was hungry, and you gave me food, I was thirsty and you gave me something to drink, I was a stranger and you welcomed me, I was naked and you gave me clothing, I was sick and you took care of me, I was in prison and you visited me" (Matthew 25:35-37). The disciples can't imagine what he is talking about, until Jesus says, "Truly I tell you, just as you did it to one of the least of these who are members of my family, you did it to me" (Matthew 25:40). And Jesus demonstrated the posture he asks of his followers by washing his disciples' feet, taking the form of a servant. Directly addressing servanthood, Jesus says, "Whoever wishes to be great among you must be your servant ... the Son of Man came not to be served but to serve" (Matthew 20:26-28).

The life of service flows naturally and inescapably from the teachings of Jesus Christ, and no congregation or disciple can avoid the direct gift and demand of God's call to love and serve others. A church without service dies like a tree with neither roots nor fruit, without nourishment or purpose.

Compassionate service marked the early church as disciples were admonished to "be doers of the word, and not merely hearers" (James 1:22). They prayed for the sick, visited the imprisoned, and marshaled their resources to provide for the needs of the poor. Paul recognized how the core practice of love defined the Christian life, "If I speak in the tongues of mortals and of angels, but do not have love, I am a noisy gong or a clanging cymbal. And if I have prophetic powers, and understand all mysteries and all knowledge, and if I have all faith, so as to remove mountains, but do not have love, I am nothing" (1 Corinthians 13:1-2). Love, incarnate in ministries of compassion, mercy, and justice, bears witness to the living Christ.

3.

So, if *mission* and *service* appropriately describe the volunteer impulses and outward reach that characterize so many our congregations, why qualify them with the adjective *risk-taking*? Vibrant, fruitful, growing congregations push beyond ordinary service and everyday missions to offer extraordinary opportunities for life-changing engagement with people.

Risk-taking steps into greater uncertainty, a higher possibility of discomfort, resistance, or sacrifice. Risk-Taking Mission and Service takes people into ministries that push them out of their comfort zone, stretching them beyond the circle of relationships and practices that routinely define their faith commitments. God uses such ministries to expose church members to people, situations, and needs that they would never ordinarily encounter and that reveal to them spiritual qualities and practical talents that, apart from their deliberate intention of serving Christ, they would never discover. The most poignant of Jesus' teachings and practices were costly demonstrations of unexpected love that transformed lives, families, communities, and the world.

Jesus says, "If you love those who love you, what credit is that to you? For even sinners love those who love them. If you do good to those who do good to you, what credit is that to you? For even sinners do the same" (Luke 6:32-33). People naturally love those who love them. Anyone with the good taste and good sense to treat me well is the kind of person I find it easy to treat well in return! People instinctually love their families and friends, those who think and live like they do, those with whom they naturally intermingle and congregate. Even unbelievers and those who never seek Christ do the same. The social cohesion of countless good political associations, civic clubs, professional organizations, neighborhood cliques, trade unions, and country clubs prove the point.

The stretch of Christian discipleship is to love those for whom it is not automatic, easy, common, or accepted. To love those who do not think like us or live like us, and to express respect, compassion, and mercy to those we do not know and who may never be able to repay us—this is the love Christ pulls out of us. Jesus stepped across oppressive social boundaries, intermingled with those who suffered crippling infirmities and social stigma, and offered hope to those at their point of gravest despair. He loved the least lovable and the most vulnerable, and he offered the same unmerited grace to the greatest sinner as to the finest saint. The down-and-out see in Christ as much love for them as the up-and-coming. And Christ invites his disciples to follow him into this kind of love.

"But love your enemies, do good, and lend, expecting nothing in return. Your reward will be great, and you will be children of the Most High; for he is kind to the ungrateful and the wicked. Be merciful, just as your Father is merciful" (Luke 6:35-36). "Do to others as you would have them do to you" (Luke 6:31).

Risk-Taking Mission and Service involves work that stretches people, causing them to do something for the good of others that they would never have considered doing if it were not for their relationship with Christ and their desire to serve him. Of course, church members love and serve those close at hand in their congregations and neighborhoods, even if these are the fruit of natural inclinations as well as commitment to Christ. But it is important to look beyond one's own close social and community circles and consider how Christ desires to use a person's gifts and talents and capacities to enhance the well-being of others beyond the inner circle.

What have we done in the last six months to make a positive difference in the lives of others that we would not have done if it were not for our relationship to Christ? Reflecting on this question takes us to another level in our understanding of Christian discipleship, moves us beyond our comfort zone, and presses us to follow Christ into more adventurous encounters with people. As we do so, God's Spirit changes us, changes others, and changes our churches. That's Risk-Taking Mission and Service.

Risk-taking also draws our attention to the truth that many of our most urgent ministries have an uncertain, unpredictable quality. We cannot know whether or not our efforts will make the difference we hope. Much of our hardest work may have little visible impact or may seem to end in utter failure. Sometimes alcoholics we help through rehab return to addictions, children we remove from violent homes run away anyway, homes we build are destroyed by the next flood, disadvantaged youth we support with scholarships drop out after two years, and ex-cons we take a chance on end up back in prison. Like the seeds scattered by Jesus' sower that land on rocky ground, get choked by weeds, or gobbled by birds, many of our finest efforts come to no visible good. But like Jesus' parable promises, as we remain faithful to the task, a harvest comes forth in miraculous ways. Christ's ministry requires our willingness to risk failure.

Lucas runs a small business, has a young family, and volunteers frequently at church. After a spiritually powerful experience on a Walk to Emmaus retreat, he prayerfully searched for ways to respond to God's call to make a difference. He did not feel called to ordained ministry, but he did want his life marked by greater service to Christ. He joined a team of men who met weekly for months to plan a prison ministry, Kairos, to offer spiritual sustenance to those serving time (kairosprisonministry.org). He and his team received permission, signed waivers, and were permitted to spend seventy-two hours in a maximum security facility for violent offenders. He describes the experience as nothing short of life-changing for himself as well as for many of the incarcerated and the other volunteers. Their significant engagement, genuine conversation, gracious respect, and active concern broke down barriers and established relationships that would extend for years. The renewed hope and deepened mutual understanding were little short of miraculous. "I was in prison and you visited me" (Matthew 25:36).

David, a pastor serving congregations and extension ministries for years, after conscientious prayer and study, concluded that capital punishment runs contrary to the teachings of Christ. He also realized how controversial and unpopular this perspective was in his own community. Public protest and signing petitions did not fit his style. Instead of trying to win consensus in his church about capital punishment (although he unapologetically teaches what he believes) and feeling frustrated by the intransigence of the criminal justice system and legislature to change, he decided to make his own personal commitment. By patiently working through the resistance of the bureaucracy of a prison near his home, he received permission to make bi-weekly pastoral visits to one of the prison's death row inmates. Every other week, he submits to the searches, completes the forms, and signs the waivers so that he can spend an hour in conversation, reading, Bible study, and prayer with a man convicted of murder who has no appeals, no options, and no hope as the world understands it. He does this consistently and without publicity or need for recognition. He holds no naïve hope of conversions or reprieve. He simply and graciously steps into the world of another person radically different from his own to offer the ministry of Christ. It's a world he would never know and never consider entering if it were not for his relationship to Christ.

After their children went off to college, four women from a suburban congregation decided to move beyond their comfort zone with their volunteer spirit. They took a one-day training for literacy tutors, contacted the pastor of a mission church in an area with low-income housing and high drop-out rate, and were introduced to several children and their mothers seeking basic literacy and English language classes. Each Friday, the four spent two hours teaching, listening, laughing, crying, and otherwise interweaving their lives with people they would otherwise never have come to know. They supported each other, worked as a team, made contacts that drew their own congregation into greater engagement with the mission church, and felt God's Spirit reshaping their perceptions about poverty, race, and language. It was a world they would never have considered entering if it were not for their relationship with Christ. Later one of the women said, "I didn't want to do it, but God pushed me through the door. I receive more than I give. Now I wouldn't trade my time with these young people for anything."

Stories abound of individuals responding to the call to address human need through Risk-Taking Mission and Service. Thousands of church people follow the common path marked by our forebears and repeated in every generation. The history of mission and service consists of successive excursions from the same starting point—awareness of human need, perceiving God's call to do something, feelings of unworthiness and inadequacy, courageous response, using spiritual gifts and material resources, overcoming resistance, opening ourselves to suffering, making a difference, discovering meaning and purpose, and inviting others.

Not everyone has the spiritual gifts, the personal temperament, or the physical stamina to step beyond the edge of ordinary service. Not everyone works the front lines where the church engages the most intransigent and difficult of society's challenges. That's all right. In the Body of Christ are many members, and "not all the members have the same function" (Romans 12:4). Those who courageously and faithfully take on bold or

90

audacious ministries for the sake of the church require the support and encouragement of many members. For Lucas to succeed with the Kairos prison ministry required financial resources, the cooking skills of a large team, the willingness of people to support his endeavor with printing materials, and the hosting skills of many other volunteers as the team prepared. This experience will become the seed for larger church engagement. Pastor David benefits from the ministry of prayer offered by his covenant group and Sunday school class. And within months of the women beginning their literacy tutoring, plans were underway for other volunteers to work alongside members of the mission church to offer Vacation Bible School. Dozens of people served by preparing meals, serving refreshments, leading music, providing transportation, and teaching.

The sharp edge of new and bold ministry often begins with the leadership of a few people, brings others into supportive roles, and then engages the whole congregation. Vibrant, fruitful, growing congregations encourage, support, and embolden those who are imaginative and adventurous in their engagement with the sufferings of the world, and then cultivate systems of support that help many more people use their talents and resources to make a difference. Such congregations offer ministries of Risk-Taking Mission and Service that invite, involve, and shape the altruistic, self-giving stirrings of its members and that sustain significant life-changing ministries in the community or world.

Never underestimate the enormous impact a church can have, even if only a small percentage of its members offer themselves for front-line, risk-taking service. Even major projects begin by God calling only one or two people to do something bold.

The Mozambique Initiative of The United Methodist Church partners more than 300 U.S. congregations with more than 170 Mozambique congregations; sustains scholarships for seminary students; digs life-saving wells in remote areas of Mozambique; provides pension support for retired African pastors; and spiritually binds two distant areas of the globe through mutual prayer, VIM projects, exchange programs, and student visits. It began with the vision of two United Methodist bishops, Ann Sherer and Joao Machado. The fruits are manifold and increasing with each year (MozambiqueInitiative.org).

The PET Project (Personal Energy Transportation) uses the work of several hundred volunteers (mostly retired) at ten different assembly sites in the U.S. to construct hand-cranked wheelchairs, providing the gift of mobility to more than two thousand people in sixty countries each year. These finely

<table>
<tr><td>

"Personal Faith and Public Policy"

Years of preaching, teaching DISCIPLE Bible Study, and working to improve others' lives convinced Rev. Steve Copley, pastor of First United Methodist Church, North Little Rock, Arkansas, that the church should take a more active voice in shaping public policy. He and his church spearheaded a campaign that worked with other congregations and faith communities to raise the minimum wage in Arkansas in an effort to help workers with full-time jobs who nevertheless live in poverty. The grassroots "Give Arkansas a Raise Now" campaign culminated in the state legislature voting overwhelmingly to support an increase of $1.10 an hour and the Governor signing the bill into law. For Copley and his congregation, the issue was one of social justice that required a response from people of faith.

</td></tr>
</table>

crafted vehicles are assembled and sent to the persons with the greatest need and the least resources throughout the world. God uses the gifts and talents of engineers, machinists, amateur woodworkers, financial supporters, and office volunteers to dramatically change the lives of people around the world. PET began with the vision and energy of one retired United Methodist pastor, Mel West, who felt called by God to help the victims of landmines and polio in underdeveloped countries (giftofmobility.org).

The Rainbow Network raises nearly two million dollars annually to provide medical care, education, housing, nutrition programs, and small business development in remote, rural areas of Nicaragua. The project recently celebrated its tenth anniversary of work to reduce suffering and poverty through self-help, Christian partnerships. The ministry thrives on the generosity and support of hundreds of congregations, individual benefactors, and volunteers. Rainbow Network began with the vision of one United Methodist layperson, Keith Jaspers, who felt God calling him to use his organizational skills, business acumen, and love for people to help the least served (rainbownetwork.org).

These three monumental projects grew from the small, initial steps taken by persons open to God's call and claim. They risked failure, resistance, and uncertainty to engage real human need, and invited others to follow. Bold ministries of Risk-Taking Mission and Service find their beginnings not just in individuals but in classes, committees, Bible studies, women's organizations, and congregations. An amazing number of long-established community-wide women's shelters, literacy centers, family clinics, crisis centers, schools, children's homes, and hospitals began because an adult Sunday school class invited a guest speaker who touched the hearts of a handful of people.

These people felt the call of God and gave themselves to the task, invited others to join and support, collaborated with other churches and community leaders, and formed a major community-wide agency to make a difference in the lives of thousands. Even the most audacious and robust community ministries began small, with a group of committed believers as common as the ones you worship and study with weekly.

Christ pulls people out of themselves and into the lives of others where they would never have gone on their own. One congregation sent one or two teams each year to clean up churches and homes after tornadoes and hurricanes. As the teams grew more confident, developed more skill, attended more training, and cultivated greater leadership, one of the teams applied and was approved as a First Responder. Now, they are not only prepared to help with clean-up during the weeks after a disaster, they are prepared to arrive first, providing immediate essentials of food, water, housing, and emotional support. Their work has blessed countless families. During each mission, the congregation surrounds them in prayer and sustains them with financial support for the equipment, travel, and expenses of this extensive ministry. The trained volunteers are not EMS technicians or firefighters but ordinary teachers, office workers, housewives, professionals, and retired folk who have let Christ push them out of their comfort zone and put them face-to-face with human suffering and need.

A small rural church with an average attendance of just over thirty people received a visitor one Sunday, a mother with a young child who had significant special needs. The child required nearly round-the-clock medical care and oversight. At first, some of the members were put off by the dramatic depth of the family's needs and disturbed by the attention the family drew. Slowly church members began to see in this family's presence a distinct call of God to help. Before long the congregation "adopted" them into their life, and adult members were trained to help care for the child so the mother could occasionally restore her strength. The few children already in the church befriended the newcomers, and men from the church alleviated accessibility issues in the adopted family's home. These acts changed the mother's life and also transformed the life of the congregation. Consistent with the mysterious economy of God, for every result one expects from an action, there are twenty results no one ever expects. Worship attendance began to increase, the spirit of the congregation became more positive, and other families with young children started attending. Congregations that risk in love and compassion attract those who seek genuine community. The switch from indifference to compassion among a few people leads to monumental change for the purposes of Christ.

A pastor of a medium-sized congregation noticed that despite her avid support of hands-on, risk-taking mission, many of her most passionate and imaginative proponents of such projects were slipping away from church involvement. She gathered a few church leaders, and they tracked how new ministry ideas worked their way through the church organization and administration to become accepted church programs. The usual pattern began with one or two people excited and energized, feeling called to meet a particular need. When they shared their idea with others, they were referred to the Missions Committee, which met three or four times a year. This meant that two months might pass before their idea received consideration. The usual business of the Missions Committee included recommending special financial offerings (hurricane or famine relief, for instance) to the Administrative Board and coordinating the Thanksgiving food basket drive and the Christmas coats appeal. Most of the committee had served for years, had little energy for hands-on projects themselves, and were simply doing what they had been asked to do: helping with the special offerings, food baskets, and coats. When a new idea was presented, they'd discuss it and conclude that they did not have money budgeted for it. They'd look around the room to see if any of the committee members were interested in leading the new effort and find no enthusiasm for the task. Several weeks later, they'd report on their discussion to the Administrative Board, where a similar dynamic took place, with none of the voting members expressing much interest. Four months would go by before projects were finally put to rest, and by that time even those who originally felt inspired had lost interest. The pastor and church leaders realized that the responses and discussions were taking too long and that the people most energized and supportive of new projects were not decision-makers serving on committees. So they devised a new plan.

Some months later, following a hurricane in a neighboring state, two members approached church leaders with the idea of forming a team of volunteers, getting some training, and traveling for a week of clean-up or repair work on homes or churches. The plan was ambitious, costly, and unlike any the church had undertaken. Instead of waiting until the next Missions Committee meeting, the pastor and the two members who had been inspired by the idea thought together about the most likely people to be interested and gifted for such a project. They personally invited these seven people together for prayer and discussion and also used the church bulletin to invite anyone else interested in the project to attend. The meeting attracted nearly twenty people. The two who had raised the original idea had done their homework before the meeting. They had contacted their denominational office on volunteer ministries to get information on how to coordinate with other congregations and how to work in cooperation with local churches in the affected area. They shared the information with the gathered group. Since the gathering included those eager to do something, they found themselves confirmed and strengthened, encouraged by others who also felt called to this work. They agreed not to ask the Finance Committee to amend the church budget. Instead they asked for permission to gather support from special offerings, Sunday school classes, and individuals eager to help. They closed the meeting with prayer and agreed to meet again the next week. Step by step they worked out the details. By the time they presented a report to the Missions Committee and Administrative Board, they had the project planned and had named a team of twelve volunteers for the project who would be supported by numerous auxiliary volunteers assisting at home with food, materials, and communication. They presented their budget, fully supported by gifts and pledges outside the existing church budget. The Missions Committee gladly supported their efforts, and the Board enthusiastically offered its blessing and approval. Thus began a new era in hands-on mission in the church, and a new style of initiating ministry.

What did the pastor and church leaders learn from the experience? First, congregations should give ready permission to those who have the energy for and interest in new initiatives. They ought to reduce the number of hurdles, the layers of organizational reporting and approval seeking, especially by persons who have no particular interest in volunteering themselves. Leadership, vision, planning, soliciting help, and participation must come from those who feel called and eager. Cultivating a permission-giving, rather than an approval-seeking, environment in a congregation has huge implications not just for the planning of missions but for beginning new Bible studies, support groups, and other ministries. Lyle Schaller once observed that when it comes to initiating new ministries, churches should "Count only the 'Yes' votes." By this he means, don't let those who have no interest in new work veto those who have the energy and inspiration to do a project because not everyone has to attend and support a project for it to be effective and life-changing. Second, the congregational leaders learned that they have to act quickly in response to serious human need in order to channel and cultivate the charitable impulses of members. Lengthy approval-seeking structures kill enthusiasm.

4.

How do churches cultivate the practice of Risk-Taking Mission and Service over and above the ordinary and necessary service and mission that characterize most congregations?

Churches that practice Risk-Taking Mission and Service not only raise money to support overseas, international, and community work, they also organize teams, solicit and train volunteers, and send people to work directly in hands-on, face-to-face ministries. They value contact, engagement, and long-term relationships, and they measure the impact of their work in lives changed rather than in money sent or buildings constructed. They don't stop at reading about the global church, they globalize their own ministry by forming partnerships with sister churches, supporting international student exchanges, and sharing common prayers. They give people multiple opportunities to serve in meaningful ways.

Such congregations go the extra mile and put forth the effort to see that the people they serve feel respected, confirmed, confident, and blessed, not dependent or helpless or indebted. They do *mission with* people of other cultures and not *ministry to* them; they don't view service as a one-way street, as if their members hold all the answers and have all the resources and are helping people who have nothing. They sharpen their sensitivity to the inequalities of power and

> ### "Church as Catalyst for Community Change"
>
> Few urban churches have had as great an impact on their cities as St. James United Methodist Church in Kansas City. Under the leadership of Rev. Emanuel Cleaver for more than twenty years, the predominantly African-American congregation has reshaped city policies and practices in housing, education, and employment and has become a center for leadership development for community issues. Not only does the church excel in advocacy and community engagement, it also offers extraordinary hospitality to visitors; reaches out to invite people in; and provides high quality, authentic, and engaging worship and music. One person remarked, "I've never seen any congregation that has made as big a difference, not only in the spiritual lives of people, but also in the quality of life of a community." It's difficult to imagine how different Kansas City would be had St. James decided simply to stay focused within its own walls, play it safe, and never risk community and political change.

wealth, and work toward partnerships and mutual ministry in which they learn as much as they teach, receive as much as they offer, and grow in Christ through their sharing of Christ's compassion. They practice humility and cultivate the fruit of the spirit in their work together and their engagement with those they serve. They expect nothing in return and do not hunger for public approbation or measure their impact by the gratitude expressed by those they help. People come first, and Christ's love for people binds them to one another and to their task.

Churches shaped by Risk-Taking Mission and Service not only solicit and encourage ordinary service to support the work of the congregation—inviting, equipping, organizing, encouraging—but they also consciously seek to motivate people to more extraordinary service. They lift examples in preaching and teaching, and they support those on the cutting edge of service with prayer, funding, and appreciation. They don't let the fear of controversy or resistance within the congregation override their support for ministries of compassion by members called to such work. They do not self-righteously criticize or belittle those members who cannot or will not work on the front lines beyond the comfort zone, but rather they work intentionally to develop ways in which everyone can play a supportive role. The spirit of mission unites them rather than divides them. They don't try to make everyone fit the same mold, and they offer mission and service opportunities with gradations of involvement and differing levels of complexity appropriate to the talents, skills, and interests of a variety of people. They don't just promote the highly-visible, time-intensive special projects but also provide ways for those who can give a few hours a week to serve. They value the person standing atop the roof on the work-site as highly as the person writing letters to the legislature at home, realizing that each is serving in his or her own way. For the person who steps forward wanting to help, there is always a place.

Churches that place a premium on Risk-Taking Mission and Service not only support the work of their members who volunteer for church-sponsored projects but also encourage, celebrate, and appreciate the service their members perform through community agencies; civic organizations; volunteer involvements with hospitals, clinics, schools, rehab centers, and probation courts. "Prayers, presence, gifts, and service" includes the service that members do for the purposes of Christ in the community as representatives of the congregation.

For churches with a culture of Risk-Taking Mission and Service, helping people in Christ's name is not merely the prerogative of adults but is a regular part of the formation of children and youth. All youth and children's ministries—Sunday school, mid-week, Sunday evening, Vacation Bible School, retreats, and camps—include teaching and experiential components that stretch compassion outward beyond the walls of the church. Youth ministries practice age-appropriate, hands-on, in-person service at nursing homes and social service centers. They invite medical workers, teachers, and project team members who have returned from international work to present programs for young people to enliven interest in the global family. And they prepare and sponsor age-appropriate, hands-on projects for junior high and high school age students, near home and sometimes far away. Faith mapped in childhood provides pathways that shape lifelong commitments. Churches with too few youth of their own collaborate with other congregations to offer high quality, cross-cultural, hands-on service opportunities that help people, reshape attitudes, and form memories.

Churches that practice Risk-Taking Mission not only offer their own projects and programs organized by their own members, they also collaborate with other churches, other denominations, civic organizations, social agencies, and non-profit groups. They form alliances and cooperate with others to provide a wider array of services. They weave the church's social concern into the networks of community service. They partner with private businesses to bring the greatest possible resources to bear to address a particular human need and to help teach and redirect community priorities. They willingly share responsibility and credit as long as quality, integrity, and effectiveness are preserved. Small churches collaborate with other churches to form work teams, combining efforts to achieve together what they cannot do alone.

Churches that cultivate Risk-Taking Mission and Service not only encourage members to volunteer for their projects but also actively invite and welcome newcomers, visitors, and the unchurched to help them in making a difference in the lives of others. Service projects become an entry point into the church and into life in Christ. Many people with no religious affiliation and no church home want to make a difference, yearn to improve the conditions of other people, and desire to make the world a better place by relieving suffering, reducing poverty, or struggling against injustice. Often they hold an image of churches as self-serving and self-absorbed, or as hypocritical. Young people in particular are searching for ways to channel their altruistic impulses into hands-on, face-to-face service that changes lives. Service isn't just for insiders and long-time members; it's a means God uses to shape faith and bind people into the Body of Christ.

Congregations that value Risk-Taking Mission and Service streamline the process by which ministries are approved, supported, and completed. They replace lengthy and rigid organizational protocols that strangle passion and turn the church inward with a permission-giving organizational environment that is agile, quick to recruit and respond, and empowering of those who passionately want to work. They continue annual and on-going projects that truly make a difference, and they work to create additional opportunities and channels of service so that the church's ministry remains fresh, new, and relevant to the changing needs of the community and world.

Congregations that practice Risk-Taking Mission and Service realize that while feeding one person at a time, building one house at a time, healing one illness at time, and counseling one prisoner at a time are vitally important, the church also has a responsibility to bear witness to wider social change. They tend to legislative policies, changes in public funding, legal proposals, and business practices with an eye for protecting the most vulnerable in society. Remembering Jesus' particular compassion for the poor and powerless, they advocate for policies that improve the lives and conditions of those who struggle at the margins of society. Even at the risk of disapproval by some, they mobilize against racism, injustice, and abuse, and they work and pray for peace. They help members

> **"This Is the Kind of Church We Want to Belong To"**
>
> The United Methodist Church in rural Saint James, Missouri, had a couple who continued to visit the congregation for several months. When the pastor invited them into membership, they said they were not ready to join. They preferred simply to visit when they wanted. In September 2006, a tornado swept through the small community, destroying several houses and businesses. The United Methodist Church immediately mobilized in response, with the small church becoming the headquarters for the Red Cross, helping find shelter for those who had lost homes, providing food and shelter for volunteers and first responders, and channeling resources from other United Methodist congregations to help.
>
> On the Sunday following the tornado, the couple who had been visiting stepped forward and joined the church, telling the pastor, "When we saw how this church responded to the victims of the tornado, we knew this is the kind of church we want to belong to." While increased membership is not the goal of Risk-Taking Mission and Service, it is frequently one of the fruits. People want to belong to churches that make a real difference in the lives of people.

stay informed about issues that affect people and encourage civic and political participation among their members. Risk-taking witness is a tool God uses to change lives, communities, and nations.

What's the opposite of Risk-taking? Safe. Predictable. Comfortable. Certain. Convenient. Fearful. These words do not describe the ministry of Jesus Christ who said, "For those who want to save their life will lose it, and those who lose their life for my sake will save it." (Luke 9:24) The practice of Risk-Taking Mission and Service reminds us that congregations are not ends in themselves; they are resources God uses to change lives and transform the world.

God places congregations in a world troubled by many challenges. Schools struggle to provide basic education, and many children fall through the cracks. Criminal justice systems are overcrowded and do little to restore people to functional, positive participation in society. Medical services are overburdened and unprepared to serve unmet needs, especially of the poor, the uninsured, and the unemployed. Immigration issues and environmental threats intensify fears. Drugs, alcohol abuse, gambling addictions, family violence, and unmitigated poverty rob people of hope. A majority of the people with whom we share the world live with incredible uncertainty because of poverty, hunger, illness, or war.

As followers of Christ, we cannot live as if these things have nothing to do with us. Christ moves us closer to suffering, not farther away. We cannot walk around obvious suffering, ignoring it and denying it like those who preceded the Samaritan down the road to Jericho. We can't moan about how somebody ought to do something. We cannot merely lift those who suffer in prayer, asking God to do for us what God created us to do for God.

Churches that practice Risk-Taking Mission and Service are dissatisfied and offended (for Christ's sake!) by the abuse of children; the suffering of innocents; the oppression of the poor; and the recurring cycles of addiction, violence, and injustice around them. They hear in the human need of their neighbors the distinct call of God. Against all odds, they figure out a response and offer themselves faithfully and genuinely, even at some cost to themselves. God uses them to transform the world.

Congregations make disciples of Jesus Christ by graciously inviting people and welcoming people with Radical Hospitality so God can reshape their lives through Passionate Worship and mature their faith through Intentional Faith Development. They discern the call of God to transform the world with the compassion of Christ through Risk-taking Mission and Service. To sustain these core processes so that the Body of Christ thrives in this generation and into the future requires the Extravagant Generosity of Jesus' disciples, and it is to that practice that we now turn.

Conversation Questions:

- What outreach ministries of your church push people out of their comfort zones to make a real difference in the lives of people? What are the ministries that require hands-on, face-to-face engagement with the needs of people that your members might ordinarily not come to know?

- How has a mission initiative or outreach ministry changed your church? How has a service project shaped your own life? What is the most unexpected place to which your faith in Christ has taken you in order to make a difference in someone's life?

- List the church outreach programs that make the greatest impact on the lives of people in your community who are not a part of your church. How do you suppose your congregation is perceived by those in the community who have the least power—the poor, the unemployed, the stranger, the hungry, the homeless, the abused, the addicted, the immigrant, the victim of violence?

CHAPTER FIVE

THE PRACTICE OF EXTRAVAGANT GENEROSITY

"You will be enriched in every way for your great generosity."
(2 Corinthians 9:11)

1.

"I'd feel better if we could go over it one more time," Matt told his wife, Keri, as they worked together preparing their talk for the next day's Consecration Sunday Service. Before they practiced their presentation again, they found themselves reminiscing about the last several years and the incredible faith journey that had brought them to this point. The next morning they would share their story about their step-by-step movement toward tithing. Just a few years ago they couldn't have imagined doing something like this.

Matt and Keri grew up in faithful United Methodist families. Though they attended youth fellowship and Sunday school, they were less active during college. After meeting each other, getting married, and settling into the community, they became involved with the church once again. Now they're in their mid-thirties with two young children. They're both professionals with moderately high incomes, even though Keri works part-time while the children are young. They live a familiar suburban lifestyle, paying for a home mortgage, two cars, and preschool for the kids.

Matt and Keri had attended DISCIPLE Bible Study together. The experience deepened their desire to learn more about the faith and to offer more of themselves in service to the church. They helped begin a new Sunday school class for people their own age, providing much of the initial hospitality. They have also helped with children's ministries, mission projects, and countless fellowship events. They love their church. Most of their closest friendships have developed through their activity in the church.

Five years ago as the church prepared for Consecration Sunday, the pastor invited Matt and Keri to write a short devotional about giving for the newsletter. Consecration Sunday is the church's fall emphasis on giving that culminates with financial pledges to support the following year's ministries. The invitation caused them to think about their giving. They felt good about the amount of their annual gifts and believed that they were giving generously, more than most couples their age. Consecration Sunday emphasized *proportional* giving with the goal of tithing. When they did the math, they realized that they were giving less than 2 percent of their annual income to God's purposes through the church. They began to explore the practice of the tithe with greater interest.

Even though they prayerfully studied the biblical roots and practices that supported the tithe, giving 10 percent simply seemed too much to expect. They had a mortgage, car payments, college savings, and retirement plans to think about. They never had money left over at the end of the month. How could they possibly tithe?

Matt and Keri prepared the devotional that year based on their reflections about Jesus' story of the widow who put two coins in the treasury, giving more than all the others because she gave out of her poverty. They wrote about how they and their fellow church members give out of abundance rather than poverty, and they challenged others to grow in giving. They also decided to increase their giving by almost half that year, pushing them toward 3 percent of their income.

The next year, Matt and Keri were asked to give announcements in church about Consecration Sunday, talking about giving and how it shapes faith. That was the year they accepted the challenge of growing toward the tithe. They increased their giving by another 1 percent of their income and decided to do that each year for several years until they tithed. Giving 4 percent involved rethinking spending habits. They looked at some of their spending patterns, such as how frequently they bought fast-food rather than eating together at home, the number of years they drove cars before replacing them, and the kinds of entertainment they did together as a family. This level of giving caused them to look at other financial matters, including their saving and investing. They made subtle, positive changes in their lifestyle. One day it occurred to Matt that their salaries usually increased by about 4 percent per year. If they saved and spent half that increase each year and used the other half to increase their giving, they could reach the tithe in three more years. That's what they did, even though they faced one year when their income slipped lower. They kept growing in their giving as a proportion of income.

Matt and Keri reached the full practice of tithing one year ago. As much as they had prayed, talked, read, and committed themselves to the tithe, nothing prepared them for the first time they actually wrote a check for 10 percent of their income and gave it to the church at the beginning of the month. Keri remembers it as a "gut check moment" in their faith journey. It seemed crazy and extravagant. They also enjoyed an incredible sense of accomplishment.

Five years after that first devotional in the church newsletter, Matt and Keri were asked to share about their journey of faith and their growth in the grace of giving. They felt privileged and humbled to share but didn't want to boast or appear self-righteous. While the journey toward tithing had been satisfying, it had not been easy.

In planning their presentation, they decided that Matt would tell the congregation about how the tithe had deepened their understanding and practice of faith. People talk about putting God first and having God at the center of their lives, but in actual practice most of a person's major decisions are made without reference to God's will or priorities, and God is really peripheral instead of central. Instead of giving God the leftovers at the end of the month, tithing is a spiritual discipline that puts God first. It's a practical way of saying, "God really is Lord of our lives, and we do not give into society's expectations, our possessions, or our appetites." Tithing takes enormous trust in God. Tithing strengthens faith.

Next, Keri would describe how tithing forced them to think about the use of money and how all they receive has been entrusted to them by God. Tithing made them spend money more wisely, with less waste and fewer superfluous or impulse purchases. Practicing the tithe caused them to save more diligently and to consider the impact their investments have on society. They looked at their money as if each dollar had a mission. As stewards, their job was to see that the money fulfilled purposes consistent with their being followers of Christ. How they spent, how they saved, and how they gave reflected this sense of mission. Tithing made them rethink their borrowing and debt. Lowering credit card and auto debts freed substantial amounts for saving and giving.

Keri would describe how, for she and Matt, tithing had broken the sense of panic, worry, desperation, and fear that had driven many of their financial decisions in the past. The knowledge that they could willingly give away 10 percent of their income relieved their feeling trapped, paralyzed, or hopeless about their financial situation. By giving more, they worried less.

Then Matt would describe how the many conversations they had about priorities, family spending habits and saving patterns, and the handling of debt had enriched their relationship immeasurably. Commitment to the tithe forced significant discussions about their goals and values as a family that they would never have had otherwise.

Finally, they would close their witness to the congregation by describing how tithing intensified their already strong engagement with the church. They became more keenly involved and interested in the well-being of the church than they ever had before. They delighted in the church's growth, the effectiveness of its ministries, and the outreach and mission. Tithing sealed and confirmed their sense of belonging to the church. They made the church's mission part of their own and prayed for the people, the ministries, and the outreach of the church with renewed passion.

Matt and Keri reviewed their talk one more time, overwhelmed by the awesome sense of change that had come over them during the last several years. They offered thanks to God and prayed God's blessing on their work as they looked forward to sharing their story in order to encourage others to grow in the grace of giving.

2.

With minor variations, Keri and Matt's story has been repeated in the lives of countless followers of Christ. First-century Christian communities, the Methodists of the 1700s, faith mentors, and models of Christian living today—all have discovered a truth as sure as gravity, that generosity enlarges the soul, realigns priorities, connects people to the Body of Christ, and strengthens congregations to fulfill Christ's ministries. Giving reflects the nature of God. Growing in the grace of giving is part of the Christian journey of faith, a response Christian disciples offer to God's call to make a difference in the world.

Keri and Matt's steps toward tithing are similar to my own, and their journey resonates with the stories of innumerable Christians of all walks of life—janitors and teachers, factory workers and small business owners, maids and executives, lawyers and farmers, wage earners and retired folks, doctors and housewives—some with incomes so small that it's difficult to imagine how they manage to give anything at all, and others with resources so large that their local church can't absorb their generosity, causing them to direct their charitable impulses toward camps, colleges, new church starts, and social service agencies.

People who give generously to the church do so because they genuinely desire to make a positive difference for the purposes of Christ and because they want to align their lives with higher purposes. They give in response to the Spirit's urging and feel a soul-sustaining satisfaction in the sense of meaning and connection that comes with generosity. They

"One of My Own"

A long-time member and proud grandfather stood at the baptismal font with his family for the baptism of his baby granddaughter. Another infant from another family that was new to the congregation was baptized at the same service. Following the service, the two families intermingled at the front of the church as they took turns having their pictures taken. At one point, the mother from the new family needed to get some things out of her bag, and the grandfather from the other family offered to hold her baby. Other church members were mixing and greeting, and several commented on the grandfather with the baby, and he found himself saying several times, "Oh, this one isn't mine; I'm just holding him for a minute."

Monday morning the grandfather called the pastor at the church office and said he wanted to see him right away. The pastor assumed the worst, thinking somehow the long-term member was upset about something from the day before. When the grandfather arrived at the church office, he told the pastor, "I want to change my will to include the church, and I want to talk to you about how to do that." The pastor was stunned and couldn't help asking about what brought the grandfather to this decision. The older man's eyes grew moist as he said, "Yesterday I realized something while I was holding that other baby, the one from the family that just joined the church. I kept telling people that wasn't my child, but then it dawned on me that it was part of my family, part of my church family, and that I have a responsibility for that little boy just like I have for my own grand-daughter. I've been a member of this church for more than forty years, and in God's eyes I'm a grandfather to more than just my own. I've taken care of my own children with my will, but I realized I also need to provide for the children of the church. So I want to divide my estate to leave a part to the church as if the church were one of my children." Those who practice Extravagant Generosity have a God-given vision and faith to plant seeds for trees whose shade they will never see.

give because they love God, love the church, and desire to grow in love of neighbor.

Vibrant, fruitful, growing congregations practice Extravagant Generosity. These churches teach, preach, and practice proportional giving with a goal toward tithing. They encourage their church members to grow in the grace of giving as an essential practice of Christian discipleship, and as a congregation they practice generosity by their extraordinary support for missions, connectional ministries, and organizations that change people's lives. They thrive with the joy of abundance rather than starve with a fear of scarcity. They give joyously, generously, and consistently in ways that enrich the souls of members and strengthen the ministries of the church.

Churches embrace newcomers with a sustaining sense of belonging when they practice Christ's Radical Hospitality. Through Passionate Worship, God shapes hearts and minds, creating the desire to grow in Christ. Through the practice of Intentional Faith Development, people make themselves available to listen for God's Word and for the Spirit to mature their understanding of God's will. Inner spiritual growth finds outward expression in Risk-Taking Mission and Service as people respond to God's call to make a positive difference in the lives of others. As people grow in relationship to Christ, they grow also in the practice of Extravagant Generosity, offering more of themselves for the purposes of Christ and providing the resources that strengthen ministry and that help the church touch the lives of more and more people in the same way their own lives have been transformed by God.

3.

Scripture is replete with examples and teachings that focus on possessions, wealth, giving, gifts, generosity, offerings, charity, sacrifice, and sharing with those in need. Giving is central to Jewish and Christian practice because people perceive God as extravagantly generous, the giver of every good gift, the source of life and love. People give because they serve a giving God.

In the Old Testament, numerous passages underscore the significance of tithing (giving a tenth) and of first fruits (offering the first and best of the harvest, livestock, and income to the purposes of God). In Genesis 14:20, Abram gave a tenth of everything to God, and throughout Leviticus and Deuteronomy, the practice of tithing and first fruits is evident. The book of Exodus says, "Take from among you an offering to the LORD; let whoever is of a generous heart bring the LORD's offering" (Exodus 35:5). Offering money and other possessions to God results from generosity of heart rather than from mere duty and obligation.

In Proverbs, people are reminded to "Honor the LORD with your substance and with the first fruits of all your produce" (Proverbs 3:9). How people use their material resources either honors or dishonors their relationship to God. Generosity aligns one's life with God's purposes.

The prophet Malachi calls upon people to rely genuinely upon God by offering the tithe, implying that when people test God's faithfulness, they find God's presence and promises trustworthy (Malachi 3:8-10). The voices of the prophets ring the warning that people cannot expect material sacrifices alone to please God but that God's reign requires justice, righteousness, and faithfulness (Amos 5:21-24; Micah 6:8).

Jesus' teachings abound with tales of rich and poor, generous and shrewd, givers and takers, charitable and selfish, faithful and fearful. He commends the poor widow putting her two coins in the treasury; giving out of her poverty, she "put in all she had to live on" (Luke 21:1-4). The story upsets expectations by pointing to proportion rather than amount as the measure of extravagance.

In the story of the farmer who built bigger barns, placing his trust too much in earthly possessions, Jesus asks the spiritually probing question, "And the things you have prepared, whose will they be?" He warns, "Take care! Be on your guard against all kinds of greed; for one's life does not consist in the abundance of possessions" (Luke 12:13-21). Acquisitiveness does not foster life rich in God.

And Jesus recounts the parable of the three servants entrusted with varying talents to illustrate God's desire for the faithful to use what has been given to them responsibly and productively. The steward who fearfully hoards and buries his talent for safe-keeping is rebuked (Matthew 25:14-30). How people use what they have matters to God.

Jesus chastises the scribes and Pharisees for hypocrisy, tithing while neglecting justice, mercy, and faithfulness. People of God are to practice justice and compassion without neglecting the tithe (Matthew 23:23). The tithe does not meet in full measure what the gift and demand of God's grace requires of Jesus' followers.

Jesus' unexpected love for Zacchaeus so radically changes the tax-collector that he gives his wealth to the poor and to those whom he has wronged. Giving serves justice and is a fruit of Christ's transforming grace (Luke 19:1-10).

Even the story of the Good Samaritan highlights extraordinary generosity. The Samaritan not only binds up the wounds of the stranger left to die in the road, but he takes the stranger to an inn, pays for the stranger's care with his own money, and commits himself to provide for the long term well-being of the stranger by telling the innkeeper, "When I come back, I will repay whatever more you spend" (Luke 10:35). The Samaritan's generosity, like Christ's compassion, knows no bounds.

Beyond all the teachings, parables, and stories, the followers of Jesus see in the gracious and costly gift of his sacrifice and death the ultimate self-revelation of God. The most memorized Scripture of the New Testament expresses the infinite nature of God's gracious love revealed in the gift we have received in Christ. "For God so loved the world that he gave his only Son" (John 3:16).

In the early church, the followers of Jesus "would sell their possessions and goods and distribute the proceeds to all, as any had need" (Acts 2:45). Generosity was a mark of the Spirit's power to change lives and practices.

Paul describes generosity as one of the fruit of the spirit, alongside love, joy, peace, patience, kindness, faithfulness, gentleness, and self-control (Galatians 5:22). He describes how "we have gifts that differ according to the grace given us," including "the giver, in generosity" (Romans 12:6-8). All Christians practice generosity while some are particularly gifted by the Spirit to give in extraordinary measures.

Paul commends the generosity of communities of faith, especially those who remain surprisingly extravagant in their giving during difficult travails. Writing of the churches of Macedonia, he says "for during a severe ordeal of affliction, their abundant joy and their extreme poverty have overflowed in a wealth of generosity on their part." They "gave according to their means, and even beyond their means, begging us earnestly for the privilege of sharing in this ministry to the saints" (2 Corinthians 8:2-4).

Paul warns those with material means not to set their hopes on the uncertainty of riches but rather on God, who richly provides everything. "They are to do good, to be rich in good works, generous, and ready to share, thus storing up for themselves the treasure of a good foundation for the future, so that they may take hold of the life that really is life" (I Timothy 6:18-19).

In every Scripture above—Abram with his tithe, the widow giving all she had, Zacchaeus in his transformation, the Samaritan with his compassion, the Macedonian church during its travails, and God's self-giving in Christ's death and resurrection—giving is always *extravagant*, life changing, and joyous.

John Wesley and the early Methodists practiced generosity as a necessary and indispensable aspect of discipleship, essential for the maturing of the soul and for the work of the church. Wesley taught Methodists to "Gain all you can, save all you can, and give all you can" ("The Use of Money," 1744). He feared that the frugality of early Methodists would lead to levels of wealth that would distract them from their growth in faithful living. Wesley warned against earning

"Scarcity to Abundance"

Six members of the Finance Committee of a small congregation faced the challenge of paying for an unexpected air conditioning repair bill of $465. The church had already exceeded its maintenance budget for the year, and account balances were dangerously low. The lay members included a retired salesman, a banker, a teacher, a housewife, a small business owner, and an insurance agent. For more than forty-five minutes they discussed options. Should they borrow the money, postpone a utility payment, make an additional appeal for money on Sunday? Should they reallocate budgeted resources from other ministries? They considered other money raising options, such as a rummage sale, a bake sale, a dinner. The thought occurred to go to one of their wealthiest members and ask for a special donation, even though the member was inactive and had not shown much inclination to help in the past. As the meeting went on, frustrations grew. Good solutions eluded them.

Finally, the teacher just shook her head at the impasse they had come to. Smiling, she suggested they simply stop talking and thinking so much and pause for silent prayer to see if God would provide another way. The others went along. After a few moments of silence, she looked around the room at her friends and fellow church members, and she said, "We all realize that any one of us could write a check for the full $465 and it would not make any major difference in our lifestyle, comfort, or financial security." With that she pulled her checkbook out of her purse and wrote a check for $465 to the church. Then she said, "Anyone who wants to join me can add their check, too, and we'll earmark the surplus for children's ministry." Three others followed her lead, and two wrote checks for $200 and $100 respectively. The result of her inspiring and generous leadership? The air conditioner repair bill was paid, and the children's ministry had an unexpected $1695 to launch a new initiative to teach the faith to the next generation!

There's no end to what the church can accomplish for the purposes of Christ when the sharp awareness of the assets, resources, and talents that God entrusts to us supercedes the fear of scarcity and the obsessive focus on needs, problems, and shortages. Extravagant Generosity means graciously and responsibly placing ourselves and our resources in service to God.

money in destructive ways, by means that corrupted the soul or contributed to injustice. He encouraged Methodists to live simply, without opulence, avoiding the waste of money on things unnecessary. Early Methodists were invited to practice self-control, self-restraint, and self-denial. Such practices deepened faith, avoided pride and vanity, and resulted in a greater capacity to help others. Generosity, according to Wesley, was rooted in grace, an emptying of oneself for others, an expression of love of God and neighbor.

4.

The practice of *generosity* describes the Christian's un-selfish willingness to give in order to make a positive difference for the purposes of Christ.

Extravagant Generosity describes practices of sharing and giving that exceed all expectations and extend to unexpected measures. It describes lavish sharing, sacrifice, and giving in service to God and neighbor.

Vibrant, fruitful, growing congregations thrive because of the extraordinary sharing, willing sacrifice, and joyous giving of their members out of love for God and neighbor. Such churches teach and practice giving that focuses on the abundance of God's grace and that emphasizes the Christian's need to give rather than on the church's need for money. In the spirit and manner of Christ, congregations that practice Extravagant Generosity explicitly talk about the place of money, in the Christian's walk of faith. They view giving as a gift from God and are driven to be generous by a high sense of mission and a keen desire to please God by making a positive difference in the world.

The notion that stewardship rightly focuses on the Christian's need to give rather than the church's need to receive is not simply a money-raising strategy but a spiritually powerful truth. The practice of tithing blesses and benefits the giver as much as it strengthens the mission and ministry of the church.

Americans live in an extraordinarily materialist and consumerist society. We are immersed in a culture that feeds acquisitiveness, the appetite for more and bigger, and that fosters the myth that self-worth is found in material wealth and that happiness is found in possessing. Thirty-year-olds feel like failures because they don't already have the kind of house and car that their parents own, and forty-year-olds feel unsuccessful because they're not millionaires. Millions of couples struggle under oppressive levels of debt that strain marriages, destroy happiness, and intensify conflict and anxiety. As one radio show host says, "We buy things we don't even need with money we don't even have to impress people we don't even know" (*The Dave Ramsey Show*).

Forty percent of the American people spend 110 percent of their annual income each year. People sustain their lifestyles through ever-increasing auto loans, credit card debt, and mortgages.

When people with different incomes are asked, "How much more income would it take for you to be happy?" they answer in surprisingly consistent ways, saying that 20 percent more income would ease their burdens, help them buy all they needed, and bring security. People earning $10,000 think an income of $12,000 will finally bring happiness, and those earning $50,000 think that with $60,000 they can finally get on top of things, and those earning $500,000 feel that with only $100,000 more income, they will finally have it made! In other words, people who earn 20 percent less than we do think they will be happy

---

"Caught Doing Good"

A downtown congregation in a moderately-sized community had occasional transients, homeless persons, and street people who would ask for handouts. Often street people would be found sleeping on the front steps. The staff developed rules, guidelines, and policies for how to help or how to refer those who asked for help. They had many discussions about the pros and cons of giving cash, vouchers, and addresses of other social agencies. One day's discussion took considerable staff time with few conclusions.

As the pastor was leaving the church later that afternoon, he noticed the part-time custodian carrying out the garbage to the large trash bin in the alley. There was a homeless person sprawled out beside the bin, looking barely conscious. As the custodian approached the trash bin, he set down the garbage bag he was carrying, reached into his pocket, pulled out his wallet, and removed a few dollar bills. Without having been asked, he walked over to the homeless person and

---

113

gave him the money, said something, then continued his work, and returned to the church. The pastor was amazed and humbled by this extraordinary display of generosity. The part-time janitor who earned less than anyone else on staff gave generously without even being asked, while the staff had spent several hours trying to figure out policies and procedures.

The pastor asked the custodian why he gave the money without even being asked and also pressed him about whether he thought the homeless person might misuse the money for alcohol or drugs. "I always do that when I can," the janitor answered. "I give them a little money and say, "God bless you," because I figure that even though they may be pretty messed up, they are some mother's son, some father's child, and so I give them something. What they do with the money—well, they have to answer to God about that. I just have to answer to God about what I do with mine."

if they can earn what we earn. So why do *we* feel discontent with what we have? Happiness based on possession causes people to pursue a receding goal, leaving them dissatisfied, wanting more, and never able to satiate their desires.

At root, these are spiritual problems, not merely financial planning issues. They reveal value systems that are spiritually corrosive and that lead to continuing discontent, discouragement, and unhappiness. We can never earn enough to be happy when we believe that satisfaction, self-definition, and meaning derive principally from possessions, and we can never trust our sense of self-worth when it rests on treasures that are material and temporal. A philosophy based principally upon materialism, acquisition, and possessions is not sufficient to live by, or to die by. At some point, followers of Jesus must decide whether they will listen to the wisdom of the world or to the wisdom of God.

As in Keri and Matt's experience, proportional giving and tithing force people to look at their earning, saving, and spending through God's eyes. It reminds them that their ultimate worth is derived from the assurance that they are children of God, created by God, and infinitely loved by God. God's eternal love revealed in Christ is the source of self-worth; true happiness and meaning are found in growing in grace and in the knowledge and love of God. Giving generously reprioritizes lives and helps people distinguish what is lasting, eternal, and of infinite value from what is temporary, illusory, and untrustworthy. The discipline of generous giving places people on the balcony, helping them look out at the consumerist society with new perspective, better able to see its traps, deceptions, and myths. The practice of generosity is a means by which God builds people up, strengthens their spirits, and equips them to serve God's purposes.

Tithing helps the followers of Jesus understand that all things belong to God and that, during their days on earth, followers are entrusted as stewards to use all they have and all they are in ways that glorify God. What Christians *earn* belongs to God, and they should earn it honestly and in ways that serve purposes consistent with being followers of Christ. What Christians *spend* belongs to God, and they should use it wisely, not foolishly, on things that enhance life and do not diminish it. What they *save* belongs to God, and they should invest in ways that strengthen society. What Christians *give* belongs to God, and they need to give generously, extravagantly, and conscientiously in ways that strengthen the Body of Christ.

One hundred and fifty years ago, if your great-grandparents were active in the faith, they tithed. Why were they able to tithe one hundred and fifty years ago, but yet we have trouble doing it today? Because they were so much wealthier than we are? The truth is precisely the opposite. We struggle with tithing because our hearts and minds are more powerfully shaped by our affluence. We find it harder to give extravagantly because our society's values shape our perceptions more than our faith's values do.

Those who are new to the faith may find the practice of tithing extremely challenging. They should take it one step at a time and grow into it over a few years. If they are so overwhelmed by debt that they struggle under an oppressive anxiety, they should first make the changes in spending and lifestyle that grant them freedom from excessive debt. (See *Money Matters: Financial Freedom for All God's Children,* by Michael Slaughter [Abingdon Press, 2006].) When they breathe more freely, they can begin to give proportionally, and grow in the grace of giving toward the tithe.

On the other hand, those who have been active in the church for twenty, thirty, or forty years and have attended worship faithfully and studied Scripture in classes and felt sustained by the fellowship of the church and offered themselves in countless ways to service in the church, but who do not tithe... I would simply challenge them to think seriously and prayerfully about why this is. Why are the other practices of the faith relevant and helpful to them, but the discipline of tithing is not? Is the avoidance of tithing a fruit of faithfulness, or the result of submission to the values of a consumerist culture?

Practice the tithe. Teach children to spend wisely, to save consistently, and to give generously. Let them learn it from their parents and grandparents so that they will be generous and not greedy, giving and not self-indulgent, charitable and not self-absorbed. Extravagant Generosity changes the life and spirit of the giver.

The practice of Extravagant Generosity also changes churches. Churches that nurture proportional giving and tithing among their members thrive. They accomplish great things for Christ, offer robust and confident ministry, and have the resources to carry out ever new and helpful missions. They escape the debilitating effects of conflict and anxiety that are the fruit of a scarcity mentality. They prosper for the purposes of Christ and make a difference in the lives of people.

Every sanctuary and chapel in which we have worshiped, every church organ that has lifted our spirits, every pew where we have sat, every communion rail where we have knelt, every hymnal from which we have sung, every praise band that has touched our hearts, every church classroom where we have gathered with our friends, every church kitchen that has prepared our meals, every church van that has taken us to camp, every church camp cabin where we have slept—all are the fruit of someone's Extravagant Generosity. We have been the recipients of grace upon grace. We are the heirs, the beneficiaries of those who came before us who were touched by the generosity of Christ enough to give graciously so that we could experience the truth of Christ for ourselves. We owe the same to generations to come. We have worshiped in sanctuaries that we did not build, and so to us falls the privilege of building sanctuaries where we shall never worship.

Generosity is a fruit of the spirit, a worthy spiritual aspiration. Generosity is the opposite of selfishness, self-centeredness, and self-absorption. To practice Extravagant Generosity requires self-control, patience, kindness, faith, and love of God and neighbor. These build us up; equip us for life and for ministry; and foster perspectives and attitudes that are sustaining, enriching, and meaningful. Giving changes both the giver and the church.

5.

One congregation's giving remained level for years even though the church had enjoyed moderate growth in attendance. Since the congregation continually initiated new ministries, the budget came under increased pressure, and church leaders grew more anxious. They decided to reevaluate their stewardship practices. For years, the congregation had held an October emphasis on church commitments, highlighting the membership pledge to support the church with "prayers, presence, gifts, and service." Each week the pastor preached on one of the four. At the end of the month, members completed cards pledging their time, talent, and service to various ministries. They also completed an "estimate of giving" card, specifying the amount they intended to give to support the church for the following year.

With consensus that old ways were not working well, the pastor and the finance committee began to look at new models to develop a culture of generosity. They read books on stewardship and giving, and they reviewed stewardship plans, packages, and kits. After much discussion, they agreed to common values. First, they would not use guilt, fear, scarcity, or shame to coerce people to give. They wanted people to feel good about giving and about growing in generosity. They wanted their stewardship emphasis to unite and energize people and make them feel engaged with the ministries of the church. Second, they would shift more responsibility for discussing giving from the pastor to lay members and would invite people who practice proportional giving and the tithe to offer testimony about growing in their faith and in their relationship to God. Third, while they would be forthright and transparent about the church's budget and financial needs, they would emphasize the Christian's need to give rather than the church's need to receive. Fourth, they would teach the scriptural practice of tithing and proportional giving, giving according to one's means. Fifth, they decided to make financial stewardship the single focus for October rather than trying to focus on all four membership commitments.

As they reviewed their options, they decided that Herb Miller's *New Consecration Sunday Stewardship Program* (Abingdon Press, 2002) reflected the values and practices they wanted to follow. Church leaders encountered some resistance from a few members who believed the church shouldn't talk about money so much. One member feared that emphasizing the tithe would scare people away. Nevertheless, the Finance Committee supported the recommendations.

This stewardship model involved preparing several letters inviting people to attend during October and especially on the last weekend for the celebration of Consecration Sunday. Lay people were recruited to plan events and to make announcements in Sunday school classes and in worship. Rather than just giving information and inviting people, the volunteers shared about the place of giving in their own faith journeys. The plan also called for the pastor to preach on giving, generosity, and tithing during October, emphasizing the Christian's need to give as well as clearly connecting giving to the mission of the church and to the lives changed by the church. At a leadership dinner, board members were asked to invite church members to attend Consecration Sunday and to stay for a Celebration Lunch. At one service, a member of the congregation presented a chart to show the patterns of giving for the congregation and encouraged people to take one step up toward tithing. Throughout the weeks of preparation, church members shared in Sunday school classes and in the church newsletter about why they give, how they have grown in giving, and how this has affected their relationship to the church and to God. On Consecration Sunday, a guest layperson and skilled church leader from another congregation preached at both services about the significance of giving in the Christian life and about the mission of the church. Members completed pledge cards during the service, consecrating them to God's service with prayer. Afterwards, everyone attended a barbecue lunch together. There were activities for youth and children during the service and lunch so that they, too, could be engaged with the practice of giving.

The congregation experienced what most churches do when they first decide to take giving seriously. They discovered that Consecration Sunday united and strengthened the church. Members felt affirmed and positive about their growth in giving, and more members than ever before increased their giving as they stepped closer to the practice of the tithe. Pledges increased by more than 30 percent from the previous year's giving. The more significant benefits were the renewed fellowship, faith, and purpose that Consecration Sunday inspired.

No congregation of any size can justify the failure to offer a high quality, positive, spiritually sound, annual emphasis to stimulate growth in giving and provide the discipline of pledging for members to support the mission of the church. No church can allow one or two negative voices on a Finance Committee to dampen giving by 30-40 percent by vetoing plans for a thorough campaign. Annual stewardship drives, done well and with a solid spiritual basis, benefit the givers as well as the church's ministry.

Annual stewardship plans for large churches may include high quality printed material; videos that connect giving to mission; memorable themes, signs, and symbols; and planning committees to prepare worship, music, dinners, communications, and work with children and youth. Small churches work on a different scale, requiring much person-to-person and group-by-group contact and conversation. The keys to effective and spiritually strengthening campaigns are the same in all churches, large and small: an unapologetic but gracious emphasis on proportional giving and tithing, an emphasis on giving in the giver's walk of faith, an emphasis on the connection of money to a compelling and clear sense of mission, an emphasis on widespread participation in planning and leading, and a heavy reliance not just on the pastor but on lay leadership.

6.

Churches that practice Extravagant Generosity don't talk in general terms about stewardship; they speak confidently and faithfully about money, giving, generosity, and the difference giving makes for the purposes of Christ and in the life of the giver. They emphasize the Christian's need to give more than the church's need for money. They teach, preach, and practice proportional giving with the goal of tithing. They use God's name accurately by appealing to the highest of life-giving purposes for giving rather than employing fear, guilt, pressure, and shame as motivation. They speak of joy, devotion, honoring God, and the steady growth of spirit that leads to greater generosity. They don't apologize, whine, groan, act embarrassed, or feel awkward as they encourage people to offer their best to God. People delight in giving. Pledge campaigns are not about money, dollars, and budgets but about mission, spiritual growth, and relationship to God. Stewardship efforts deepen prayer life, build community, unite people with purpose, and clarify mission. People feel strengthened and grateful to serve God through giving.

Extravagantly Generous congregations emphasize mission, purpose, and life changing results rather than shortages, budgets, and institutional loyalty. They provide a compelling vision that invites people to give joyously, thereby finding purpose, meaning, and satisfaction in changing lives. They know that God moves people to give in order to find purpose and to accomplish things for Christ. They connect money with mission.

Churches that cultivate Extravagant Generosity hold high quality annual pledge opportunities with wide participation, excellent preparation, and numerous opportunities for lay involvement and leadership. While pastors provide leadership through preaching, teaching, and example, congregations rely heavily on the witness of extravagantly generous lay persons through testimonies, sermons, leadership talks, newsletter meditations, and website devotionals. They invite into leadership laypersons who speak with integrity because of their own personal growth in the practice of giving, including people of diverse ages and backgrounds.

119

Vibrant, fruitful, growing congregations focus on stewardship during the season of annual pledging, but they also emphasize faithful giving throughout the year in preaching, Bible studies, and Sunday school classes. They speak in spiritual terms about the place of wealth, affluence, acquisition, materialism, selfishness, generosity, and giving. They do not avoid major capital funds campaigns, and they enter into major projects with excellence, professional preparation, and outstanding communication. They regularly offer members the opportunity to support special appeals and new projects, knowing that giving stimulates giving; and they've learned that when special giving is aligned with the purposes of Christ, it does not diminish support for the general budget. They readily encourage charitable contributions and philanthropic giving by their members to community service agencies and to cultural, medical, and advocacy causes that make a difference in lives of people.

Pastors who nurture the practice of Extravagant Generosity express appreciation to people who give. They thank members collectively and personally, and give God thanks for increases in giving. They send personal notes of appreciation for special gifts and for unexpected increases in giving or pledging. Through quarterly reports of giving, churches that cultivate generosity keep members informed in positive and consistent ways about their pledges and their giving. These churches excel in accurate communication about giving. In every report on a member's personal giving record, there is a tone of appreciation, a reminder of the significant difference the donor's gift makes, and a focus on the mission of changing people's lives. When members inquire at the church office or with the treasurer about their giving records, responses are quick, positive, and accurate, never defensive, confusing, or delayed. Pastors, staff, and volunteers strive to cultivate trust, appreciation, and confidence with contributors.

Extravagantly Generous churches do more than encourage, teach, and support personal generosity. They practice extraordinary generosity as a congregation, demonstrating exemplary support for denominational connectional ministries, special projects, and missions in their community and throughout the world. They take the lead in responding to disasters and unexpected emergencies. Lay and pastoral leadership view "giving beyond the walls" as indispensable to Christian discipleship and to congregational mission and vitality. They look for more and better opportunities to make a positive difference in the lives of people through congregational support and outreach. They develop mission partnerships; support agencies that help the poor; and fund mission teams, scholarships, service projects, new church starts, and other ministries that transform people's lives. They make the mission of the church real, tangible, and meaningful. Their reputation for generosity extends beyond the congregation into the community and conference.

Churches that grow in giving know that generosity increases with participation in ministry and community, and so they work to deepen the core ministries of worship, small group learning, and mission. They know that many churches do not have enough money because they don't provide sufficient ministry and mission. Rather than becoming obsessed with income, survival, and maintenance, they continually return their focus to changing lives, reaching out to new people, and offering significant mission. By growing in ministry, giving increases.

Congregations that practice Extravagant Generosity address the challenge of growing in giving to long-term members as well as to adults who are new to the faith. They also teach, model, and cultivate generosity among children and youth. Sunday school classes, after-school children's ministries, Vacation Bible School, and youth ministries all offer opportunities to give individually and to work together in groups to achieve a ministry goal that is significant, tangible, and compelling. Rather than collecting offerings in a perfunctory way, children's and youth leaders explain, teach, and connect the action of giving to the work of God. Children and youth are taught about responsible earning, spending, saving, and giving. Parents are encouraged to teach their children how to give. Congregations equip parents with ideas, suggestions, and practices that foster generosity for children and youth of all ages.

Congregations that cultivate generosity invite young adults into leadership and planning. They consider contrasting patterns of earning, spending, and giving between the generations. They accommodate the church's receiving methods for gifts and pledges to the "cashless and checkless" lifestyles of members who depend upon debit cards, online banking, and wire transfers.

Churches that take seriously the growth of giving as a spiritual discipline offer ministries that help people understand and cope with the risks of a materialist and consumerist society. They offer seminars, workshops, and retreats that help people deal with excessive debt, financial planning, estate planning, or preparing wills. Some offer support groups for those struggling with bankruptcy, compulsive gambling, or unemployment. Others cultivate practices of simplicity, socially conscious investing, and environmental responsibility. The followers of Jesus are immersed in the wider culture, and churches that teach the practice of giving as a spiritual discipline feel an obligation to relate spiritual truths to everyday challenges and choices.

The pastoral and lay leadership of churches that practice Extravagant Generosity constantly learn and adapt and improve their method of communication and teaching about giving. They attend workshops, read the literature, use consultants, study Scripture, learn about social trends and patterns of giving, and collaborate with other churches. These actions help them learn new techniques and, more importantly, deepen their theological understanding of giving, foster the charitable impulse, and inspire philanthropy.

Churches that cultivate Extravagant Generosity not only provide their members opportunities for annual giving and special offerings to support the church's ministries, they also encourage and teach members to consider legacies, bequests, endowment giving, and estate planning. They remind members of the importance of supporting the church in their wills and estate planning. They make legacy giving easy, providing information and means for people to prayerfully name the church as beneficiary of special gifts. They find ways to express appreciation for those who include the church in their planning. Pastors develop a comfortable willingness to initiate conversations with long-term members about planned giving. Such churches realize that future ministry rests upon the generosity of present members.

Churches that nurture the practice of Extravagant Generosity take seriously the stewardship of the resources entrusted to them by their members. They take extraordinary precautions to protect the integrity of their financial systems by providing proper checks and balances for those who handle money, preparing regular and accurate financial reports for church leaders and for anyone who requests them, and furnishing annual audits to appropriate trustees and financial officers. They operate with transparency, knowing that trust is the currency of financial leadership in the church and that confidence in the motives and competence of staff and volunteers is essential in order to cultivate giving. Pastors and designated laity know the financial details, cash balances, giving patterns, and church budget and are able to communicate thoroughly and accurately about the financial health of the church.

In churches that practice Extravagant Generosity, the pastor tithes. Lay leaders tithe or give proportionately with the goal of tithing. Proportional giving with the goal of tithing, regardless of income, becomes an expectation for those who serve on the Finance Committee and in other key leadership roles of the church. The spiritual maturity that comes from growth in giving and the extraordinary engagement that results from tithing bring clarity of purpose and greater integrity to all the church's ministries.

The practice of Extravagant Generosity is the fruit of maturation in Christ, the result of God's sanctifying grace that molds our hearts and changes our values and behaviors. Extravagant Generosity supports the other four practices, helping the church fulfill its ministry to make disciples of Jesus Christ in robust and fruitful ways, opening the message of God's love in Christ to more people now and for generations to come.

Conversation Questions:

- How do you feel about how your church teaches about money? What values and themes guide your church's efforts to encourage giving and tithing? How do you feel about how faithful your church is with its money?

- How has someone else's generosity touched you and shaped your practices of giving? From whom did you learn generosity? Who continues to influence you toward greater generosity?

- What's the most fun you've ever had giving money? What made the experience delightful, memorable, and meaningful? How do you feel about giving to the church's ministry?

Group Activity:

Have your group or class members list what they perceive to be the four most important core values of the congregation—the essential and enduring tenets that are so fundamental that they must be kept no matter what the circumstance. Then list the four most dominant values of American culture as reflected in magazines, television, advertising, business, celebrity culture, sports, politics, and fashion. Talk about how these contrasting values influence decisions about money, giving, and faith.

CHAPTER SIX

EXCELLENCE AND FRUITFULNESS

"My Father is glorified by this, that you bear much fruit and become my disciples." (John 15:8)

1.

To fulfill the ministry of Christ, congregations must change and grow and adapt in ways that are purposeful, thoughtful, and faithful. Change is not easy. People do not fear change as much as they fear loss, the letting go of comfortable and familiar patterns, behaviors, and attitudes. Change for the sake of change or to preserve the institution is not sufficient. Change takes many forms, and each congregation must find its own path.

By repeating, deepening, expanding, and improving upon the five basic practices of congregational ministry, churches change and grow and learn. Pervaded by the purpose of making disciples of Jesus Christ for the transformation of the world, they discover new life, readily giving up the patterns that have limited ministry and eagerly taking up those that invite people into relationship with God. They open themselves to being reshaped by God's Spirit, revived and reformed to serve the ever-changing contexts and needs of people. As they welcome and receive new people who grow in faith and in the practice of love, congregations breathe anew with an invigorating and animating sense of confidence and future.

2.

Six years ago, two United Methodist Churches were located about nine miles apart, and both together had an average attendance of slightly under a hundred people. Both churches struggled to pay full-time salaries and benefit packages for their pastors, and both were dealing with deteriorating buildings that were becoming costlier to maintain. One congregation had only a few younger families, and the other, which had more, was struggling to keep them. While attending a parent-teacher conference, a member from one of the struggling churches visited with a member from the other, each expressing frustration and despair about the future of their congregations. One suggested, "We ought to merge the churches or try *something* different. Maybe we can do more together than apart." Thus began a buzz of conversation and serious assessment in both churches.

Before long, they invited a consultant from the denomination into the conversation. He advised against a merger but proposed something much more radical. He suggested that both churches close and that members from each former church work with the conference to start a new congregation. "Dying in order to live again" sounds like a theologically sound idea, but the concept didn't seem practical or helpful to either congregation. The consultant provided demographic reports, and members learned that they lived in a rural county with a population of 14,000 people with a per capita income nearly half of the state average, making the county among the poorest in the state. Approximately one-third of the people in the county were connected to churches, another third were loosely related to congregations (Christmas and Easter people), and another third had no church affiliation at all. The members of both churches were asked to pray about these new ideas and mull over the suggestions and reports.

Each congregation sent representatives to visit other churches with similar past experiences and which were organized following the closure of nearby congregations. Church leaders did their homework, considered costs, problems, property matters, and congregational identity issues. They also dreamed about the possibilities, the resurgence in spirit, and the potential of reaching new people. They had many conversations between the two churches and many debates within each congregation. Eventually, both developed a consensus that the plan should be pursued.

Some months later, each congregation entered periods of celebration and thanksgiving about their church history and ministry. They each held final services and closed the doors of their churches for the last time. Their

126

pastors were appointed to other churches and moved to other parts of the state. Church members felt excited and fearful, hopeful and cautious. They grieved the losses that came with their decisions: the closing of treasured sanctuaries, the letting go of their unique identities, and the loss of their distinctive worship communities.

A new pastor was assigned to the area and given the task of starting a new congregation. The pastor was in his early fifties, had an effective career in ministry, and now began to research new church starts. He willingly submitted to a variety of training events, workshops, and seminars on starting new congregations, evangelism, communications, and other related topics. Within a few months, the new church was launched. While many people came from both the former congregations, the newly formed church also attracted people who had no church affiliation. Leaders identified land for purchase that provided excellent location, visibility, and accessibility to people throughout the region. They built their first phase of buildings, including a multipurpose worship space, creatively decorated children's rooms, a commercial-grade kitchen, and offices. They constructed a steel metal building not only to reduce costs but also because, as one member says, "Many unchurched people feel intimidated by formal churches and are more comfortable walking into a building like this. John Wesley preached outdoors in the fields to reach people, and we figured we could reach people best in this part of the country with a simple, functional building." Virtually every decision about the location, the building, the meeting times, the signs, and the website was shaped by a growing passion to reach people who had no church home. Congregational leaders were exhilarated with a sense of purpose: "to present the unchanging gospel of Christ in innovative ways to a changing culture."

Four years after launching, Trinity United Methodist Church in Piedmont, Missouri averages 250 people in worship, with as many as 400 attending special services on Easter and Christmas. The church's most recent Vacation Bible School served nearly 200 young people. The children's ministry is the talk of the county. Church members take the practice of hospitality to the extreme by contacting, inviting, and assimilating visitors into their ministries. Worship is casual and simple, but wonderfully authentic, powerful, and passionate. Each fall, in addition to the ongoing Bible studies and small group ministries, they offer a church-wide study to connect everyone into groups for faith formation. Most recently, they used *Transformed Giving* (Abingdon Press, 2006). The congregation actively supports global missions and seeks ways to use the gifts and talents of the congregation in service to others. Even though the church serves one of the poorest counties in Missouri, its per capita giving exceeds many congregations in the most affluent areas of the state. They have grown in attendance in a county with a stable population, initiated new ministries, and built new buildings in an area with low incomes and fixed salaries. Members of the former churches, many in their senior years, have helped create a thriving ministry to children and youth. In exemplary ways, they have practiced Radical Hospitality, Passionate Worship, Intentional Faith Development, Risk-Taking Mission and Service, and Extravagant Generosity. The result is a vibrant, fruitful, growing congregation that makes disciples of Jesus Christ.

Visiting with the lay members of Trinity, I'm struck by their passion for reaching others and their confidence about the future. They constantly talk about what the church will be like five or ten years in the future as their ministry expands. "We love our pastor," one member said, "but we realized from the beginning that this effort belonged to us. God gave us this vision and this work, and we're glad to have a pastor who's willing to go along and help us get there."

If new life, purpose, confidence, and fruitfulness can come to a congregation in rural Piedmont, Missouri, it can happen anywhere.

3.

The Missouri Conference of The United Methodist Church is comprised of 900 congregations. Twenty percent of the conference's worship attendance is found in 21 of the largest congregations. Twenty percent of the attendance is also found in 570 of the smallest congregations. The 21 largest churches grow at a rate of about 4 percent each year. The 570 churches are declining at about 6 percent a year. Nearly 70 percent of the congregations report worship attendance that is remaining the same or declining, and most pastors have never served in congregations that have reported growth in attendance during their tenure.

The median age of members in The United Methodist Church is fifty-eight years, while the median age of the population of Missouri is thirty-six. In many churches, people in their fifties are among the youngest members. Statewide census figures for Missouri show that 24 percent of the population is under the age of eighteen. If the composition of our congregations matched the population we serve, then churches with 200 people in attendance would have 50 children present, and churches with a

1000 members would see nearly 250 children running through their buildings!

Over the last forty years, the number of United Methodists in Missouri has declined by over 80,000 people while the state population has increased by close to 30 percent during the same period. There are about 150 fewer United Methodist churches in Missouri now than forty years ago. Where did all the people go? They didn't all get mad and leave; they just grew old and died, and no one took their place. The decline has not been a backdoor problem but a front-door problem. We've failed to bring new people into our churches, and we've done poorly at passing along the faith to the next generation.

Before readers judge Missouri United Methodism, they should know that the statistical trends and demographic realities of the Missouri Conference place it in the middle of the pack among conferences of The United Methodist Church in the United States. More than half the conferences in the U.S. report more dismal statistics than these, and of the half whose numbers look better, only a small handful report actual growth in membership and attendance and increasing numbers of congregations.

Something must change. United Methodist congregations cannot continue to do what they have been doing and expect downward trends to turn around. For many churches, the rising median age of membership, the increasing personnel and facility costs, and the declining attendance have reached a point where they no longer have the people or financial resources to radically change directions.

It's becoming more difficult for United Methodists to ignore the prescient words of our founder, John Wesley, who wrote in 1786, "I am not afraid that the people called Methodists should ever cease to exist in Europe or America. But I am afraid, lest they should only exist as a dead sect, having the form of religion without the power" ("Thoughts Upon Methodism").

Answers will not come in easy-to-use new programs, through quick fixes, or by adopting new slogans. Blaming, scape-goating, denying, justifying, or ignoring have not helped and are unlikely to provide positive outcomes. The most substantial threats to the church's mission do not come from the seminaries, the bishops, the general boards, the complexity of our ordination process, the apportionment system, the guaranteed appointment, or the conflicts between conservatives and liberals, although all these deserve careful attention if the church is to move toward a new future. The most significant threats come from the failure to perform the basic activities of congregational ministry in an exemplary way.

Developing a congregational culture of genuine hospitality, authentic worship, meaningful faith development, life changing outreach, and extraordinarily selfless generosity requires a profound change in attitudes, values, and behaviors for most churches. Change does not happen quickly or without pain. And yet across the connection there are hundreds, and perhaps thousands, of churches like Trinity United Methodist Church in Piedmont, Missouri that have experienced profound renewal and new life.

Churches can change. By the grace of God, churches can step out in faith in radical new directions. They can chart a future that is different from the recent past. Their ability to become vibrant, fruitful, growing congregations is directly related to their willingness to perform the five practices in a consistently exemplary way.

4.

Radical Hospitality. Passionate Worship. Intentional Faith Development. Risk-Taking Mission and Service. Extravagant Generosity. These five practices are so critical to the success of congregations that failure to perform them in an exemplary way leads to the deterioration of the church's mission. Ignore any one of these tasks or perform any of them in a mediocre, inconsistent, or poor manner, and the church will eventually decline, turn in on itself, and die away.

Vibrant, fruitful, growing congregations do not merely perform these practices adequately; they perform them in an exemplary way, constantly learning, improving, and excelling. Fruitfulness and excellence characterize every ministry of the church. Fruitfulness as a metaphor for the fulfillment and realization of purpose is deeply embedded in our faith history. The Scriptures are full of stories about fields and harvests, vines and branches, stumps and shoots, trees and figs. These give us a faith language for understanding effective Christian leadership and provide rich images for learning about the outcomes and consequences of our faith aspirations, commitments, and work.

The expectation of fruitfulness begins in the first chapter of Genesis when God says to human beings, "Be fruitful and multiply." Human fruitfulness is response to God's bounteous fruitfulness in making the heavens and the earth and all that is within them. The expectation of fruitfulness extends to the last chapter of Revelation, in which the author describes a new creation with a river of life flowing through the holy city. On each side of the river is the tree of life with twelve kinds of fruit, producing fruit each month, and its leaves are for the healing of the nations.

Jesus teaches fruitfulness through stories and sayings in all four Gospels. In Matthew, Jesus describes a disciples' life in terms of fruitfulness. He says, "Every good tree bears good fruit, but the bad tree bears bad fruit…Every tree that does not bear good fruit is cut down and thrown into the fire. Thus you will know them by their fruits" (Matthew 7:17-20). The difference someone makes stems from interior qualities of character, motive, and relationship to God.

Mark tells of Jesus feeling hungry, seeing a fig tree, and cursing its lack of fruitfulness (Mark 11:12-14). Luke records the parable of the farmer who scattered seed across the ground. Some fell on rocks, some dried out, and some were choked by weeds, but those that fell on good soil grew, producing an abundant harvest. Jesus says, "Let anyone with ears to hear listen!" (Luke 8:4-8). Despite inevitable obstacles and failures, disciples work steadfastly and with hope, trusting the God of harvest.

In John's Gospel, Jesus describes the relationship between life in God and fruitfulness. "I am the vine, you are the branches. Those who abide in me and I in them bear much fruit, because apart from me you can do nothing…My Father is glorified by this, that you bear much fruit and become my disciples" (John 15:5-8).

The disciples of Jesus bore much kingdom fruit. They healed, taught, and served. They confronted evil, sought justice, and acted with mercy. They offered God's forgiveness and proclaimed God's reign. They changed lives, carrying in their words and work the message of God's love in Christ, and forming communities of followers. The gift of the Holy Spirit was in them because they were connected to God through Christ. Life in Christ and fruitfulness are inextricably bound together.

As John Wesley established the practices that gave rise to the life changing ministries of early Methodism, he sprinkled his teachings and writings with clear expectations of fruitfulness. For those persons considered for preaching and leadership, Wesley's questions were frequently simplified to, "Is there faith? Is there fire? And, are there fruits?"

Wesley demanded evidence of grace, gifts, and fruit in ministry. The early Methodist examination question, "Have they grace for ministry?" focused on candidates' knowledge of God's pardon and love, their desire for nothing but God, and their experience of the sanctifying presence of

God. "Have they gifts as well as grace for the work?" led to consideration of candidates' natural abilities and acquired talents, their sound understanding and faculty for communicating justly, readily, and clearly.

"Have they fruit in their ministry?" was Wesley's way of probing effectiveness and evaluating what a person's work yields for God's kingdom. "Have they convinced or affected anyone, such that they have received the forgiveness of God and a clear and lasting understanding of the love of God? Is the person an instrument of God's convincing, justifying, sanctifying grace?" Wesley expected Methodist preachers and leaders to be spiritual, talented, and effective.

Fruitfulness for congregations means effectiveness in fulfilling the mission and purpose God has given them. The mission of The United Methodist Church is to make disciples of Jesus Christ for the transformation of the world. How fruitful are congregations in this task?

Congregations fulfill this purpose by performing the five practices in an exemplary fashion: through Radical Hospitality, congregations reach out and offer the invitation and welcome of Christ; God shapes hearts and minds through Passionate Worship, creating a desire for closer relationship to Christ; through Intentional Faith Development, God's Spirit helps people grow in grace and in the love of God and neighbor; maturing in Christ causes people to respond to the needs of others as they discern God's call, which results in Risk-Taking Mission and Service; and as people continue to grow in grace, they place more of what they are and what they have under the lordship of Christ, practicing Extravagant Generosity. These practices are presented in order of thinking rather than in a necessary and distinct sequence since God's prevenient, justifying, and sanctifying grace are at work at every stage of faith, and people experience all of these in varying degrees throughout their faith journeys.

If this is the way United Methodist churches fulfill their mission to make disciples of Jesus Christ, then how are we doing? Are we fruitfully and faithfully allowing God to work through us to make the difference in the lives of people?

Despite the common use of fruitfulness in Scripture and in Wesleyan practice, many people respond negatively to applying it to churches. They argue that ministry isn't reducible to objectively measurable numbers and results and that one can't quantify effectiveness in church life. They believe that pastors and congregations aspiring to visible growth are being seduced by American culture's idolization of size and competition and that faith communities that adapt to cultural change in order to appeal to people necessarily compromise core spiritual teachings.

While fruitfulness cannot be reduced to numbers, nevertheless numbers are important. Numbers represent people—each number stands for a person who is old or young, married or single, new to the faith or long-established, rich or poor, immigrant or citizen. Each is someone's son or daughter, brother or sister, father or mother, friend and neighbor. Each is a person for whom Christ died. In Christ, each is a brother or sister to every one of us. Each is a person searching for meaning; needing community; and wrestling with hope and despair, joy and grief, life and death. Each has a story, a history, and a future that are infinitely important in God's eyes. Each is a person with whom God desires to have a relationship, and God has breathed life into congregations in order to reach him or her. How do we know three thousand persons were added to the community of the church in the days after Pentecost? (Acts 2:41) Because someone thought it was important enough to notice and to keep a record of for two thousand years! If numbers are not important, then people are not important.

And while many may reject efforts to explicitly quantify effectiveness in congregational life, most people intuitively value growth in ministry. When members think together about the future of their congregation, what do they hope their community of faith will look like fifteen years into the future? What do they think their church would look like if all their highest hopes, most fervent prayers, and hardest work came to fruition beyond all expectations? Would the church have fewer people, fewer youth and children, and no new members? Would the church be weaker, smaller, older, and ready to close its doors? Of course not. Implicit in people's hopes and hearts is the desire to pass along the faith to others who come behind them and to succeeding generations. People yearn for their congregations to be alive, thriving, full of young people, confident about the future, and making a difference in the lives of more and more people.

Not all churches should seek to be megachurches, and not all churches will be large. Congregations should not consider themselves failures if they are not huge. God uses all sizes and shapes of faith communities to reach people. But faithfulness to God demands that churches invite new people, cultivate the faith among the next generation, share the good news of Jesus Christ, and change the lives of more and more people around them.

Sunday school classes, choirs, and other small group ministries that are declining or that reach the same people now as they did ten years ago should ask themselves why this is. With an awareness of the scriptural expectation of fruitfulness, they might ask themselves how they can change their practices to invite, receive, and deepen the faith of more people who do not attend any church. If they are unwilling to change the habits and attitudes that keep their group from growing, they should consider how they can use their gifts and leadership to help start other groups. How else will the faith that sustains them continue beyond their lifetimes?

Occasionally someone argues, "God desires faithfulness, not fruitfulness." Whoever suggests this might benefit from an evening of study with a Bible and a concordance, looking up references to fruit, harvest, sowing, vines, and seeds. Fruitfulness is clearly expected of Christian disciples. Jesus' teachings consistently present the expectation that his followers are stewards and that when God has entrusted them with something, God expects them to return what has been entrusted and more. All pastors and lay persons step into congregations at one point in the congregation's life and then step out at another after some years or decades of participation and leadership. Some are involved in a congregation for one or two years and then move away, and others spend a lifetime in the same church. God entrusts congregations with the ministry of Christ and "has given us the ministry of reconciliation" (2 Corinthians 5:18). When we leave a congregation (whether by moving away, illness, or death), is that congregation stronger than when we arrived? God expects fruitfulness as well as faithfulness.

Fruitfulness and faithfulness are not mutually exclusive. If the only way to remain faithful is to devalue fruitfulness, or worse, if fruitfulness indicates lack of faithfulness, then where does this take us in our thinking? Then the crowds who gathered to hear the Sermon on the Mount and the five thousand who waited all day for Jesus to break bread would prove Jesus' unfaithfulness, providing evidence that he was pandering, compromising, and watering down the gospel. John Wesley and the early Methodists would be wildly suspect; the rapid growth of the Methodist movement would prove that the gospel was tainted, diluted by culturally appealing expressions. The people who founded the congregations where we now belong and who built the buildings where we now worship would be unfaithful if we think faithfulness and fruitfulness are mutually exclusive.

Not all churches can be equally fruitful, and not all fruitfulness looks the same. Another bishop shared with me her perceptions of fruitfulness. She described how sometimes one has to climb up the tree, shinny out onto a limb, and reach far out into the branches to get just one apple. Other times, one simply has to shake the trunk and pick up what falls. And at other times, without ever touching the tree, an abundance of apples falls, piling up at one's feet

What the story of apple picking suggests about discipleship is true. There are situations where every small step toward fruitful ministry in Christ's name comes slowly and at the cost of great effort, careful strategy, and high risk. There are other situations where the harvest is so evident that we should ask God's forgiveness for not having done more in a season of readiness.

And fruitfulness takes many forms—the growing care for one another in a congregation given to conflict, the deepening faith of a group that matures in Christ together, the increasing effectiveness of a mission initiative that changes lives. Even in these contexts, growth in love, faith, and service does not justify neglecting the God-gven task to invite and involve others and to share with them the good news that God has met our highest hopes and deepest needs in Jesus Christ.

Recently, I attended a retirement service for a pastor who had served United Methodist congregations for nearly six decades. One of those honoring his ministry said, "Every time he handed in his keys at the end of an appointment to a church, the church was stronger and the ministry greater than when he had first been given the keys at the beginning." Fruitfulness and faithfulness complement and support each other.

Is it fair to expect fruitfulness in congregations and to hold one another accountable to fulfill the tasks that lead to fruitful ministry? Is it fair to propose goals that explicitly express a desire to increase ministry? Not only is it fair, it is also faithful and necessary.

To use the language of fruitfulness causes congregations to become clearer about desired outcomes. When congregations are unclear about outcomes and objectives, they resort to measuring inputs, efforts, and resources in order to evaluate success in ministry. A church with two hundred members may claim that youth ministry receives high priority and is a strength of their congregation. They may consider themselves wonderfully successful with youth. They justify their evaluation by describing that they have a full-time youth director, four great volunteer youth sponsors, an excellent gymnasium and youth room, a youth van, and a generous budget for youth trips. But what if only six youth attend? Suppose none of these youth learns to pray, becomes familiar with Scripture, helps with worship, or serves on a mission project. The church is measuring input rather than fruitfulness to assess strength. Fruitfulness directs our focus to what we accomplish for God's purposes and corrects the tendency to congratulate ourselves for all the work, resources, and people we apply to a task while ignoring or denying that our efforts may be making little difference. Focusing on fruitfulness keeps us faithful to purposes, and makes it more difficult to justify and defend ineffective or unproductive ministries.

The language of fruitfulness helps congregations align their resources and focus their efforts on reaching "more people, younger people, and more diverse people" (Lovett H. Weems, Jr., *Circuit Rider*, March/April, 2006). United Methodists pray to God for more people, younger people, and more diverse people in our congregations, seeking the guidance of God's Spirit. And yet we cannot ask God to do for us what God created us to do for God.

More people—For some reason, we hesitate to express this so directly. But if we believe that the Christian faith can help people grow in relationship to God and that it can make a difference in the world, why would we not hope that more people experience the faith? I yearn for more people worshiping God in churches and homes, more people studying God's Word in classes and retreats, more people offering themselves in service and mission to others locally and around the world, and more people speaking out for justice and on behalf of the vulnerable. My highest desire is that through our churches, more people learn the stories of the faith and grow in their understanding and experience of forgiveness, compassion, and love and that more people feel the sustaining presence of Christ through times of joy, grief, decision, and hardship. I pray for more people to develop the qualities of prayerfulness, service, kindness, gentleness, and generosity, and that more people live with hope and joy. I pray that more people offer themselves in service to relieve suffering, correct injustice, and change lives.

We should never apologize that we pray and work for more people to experience and share our ministry in Christ's name. This desire is unselfish; it is a purpose worth pouring our lives into, and it is the central purpose of the church. To desire more people in our churches does not make us fundamentalist, small-minded, aggressive, strident, or intrusive. This is a desire for which our churches should be fervent, passionate, open, and unceasingly invitational. Jesus' teachings are laced with imperatives: "Go... Tell... Teach... Do... Love... Follow... Welcome..." Jesus' words are gracious, respectful, and loving, but they are imperatives nonetheless. They leave little room for misunderstanding his urgency for us to work on his behalf to reach more people.

Younger people—Imagine a church that decides reaching younger people is vital. Does it form a new committee? Maybe. But what if the task of rethinking ministry with younger people became the mission of *every* committee of the church? We must become intentional about adapting *all* our ministries and methods to become more relevant and helpful to younger people. We must invite younger people into leadership and ministry with us. We have much to learn. But would God have it any other way than for us to give our hearts full of Christ's love to those in succeeding generations? Jesus reminds his disciples never to hinder the children as they seek him (Luke 18:16), and he speaks words of warning about those who cause little ones to stumble (Luke 17:2). Are our systems helping or hindering, inviting or providing obstacles to faith for younger generations?

A special focus on younger people does not deny or neglect ongoing ministries to people of all ages. Rather it draws attention to the fact that for most congregations, the segments of the population that are most absent and least served are children, youth, and adults under forty. Most of these will not get involved with congregations that shape all their ministries to fit the needs of people already present, namely older adults. For churches to reach younger people requires special effort, adaptation, and change.

More diverse people—So many congregations no longer match the communities they serve. Recently, a church discovered that nearly 10 percent of households in its community were headed by single mothers. But single moms comprised only about 1 percent of the congregation. Knowing that information gives us a clear notion of how God might be calling that church to focus its ministry more intentionally toward single moms. The more a congregation slips away from matching the community it serves— in median age, ethnic diversity, income, and educational levels—the more it turns in on itself and the smaller its impact for the purposes of Christ. A church that continues to focus all of its energy on a single, shrinking sliver of the social spectrum will eventually die. Churches that expand ministry to reach a greater range of people across social, economic, age, ethnic, income, and educational niches will faithfully and fruitfully thrive.

To reach more people, younger people, and more diverse people requires congregations to change their systems, practices, and attitudes.

They pour themselves into the task with extraordinary intention, energy, and creativity. They stop making excuses, break through complacency, and open themselves to a greater future. They offer ministry that is radical, passionate, intentional, risk-taking, and extravagant. They perform the critical practices of hospitality, worship, faith development, mission and service, and generosity in exemplary ways. Remember: If this can happen in Piedmont, Missouri, it can happen anywhere.

5.

Vibrant, fruitful, growing congregations also place a high premium on excellence in ministry. They do not settle for mediocrity, indifference, or a tolerable adequacy. In all five congregational practices, they offer their best and highest; they continually learn and improve and evaluate and adapt. They exceed expectations; outdo themselves in their enthusiasm for quality; and offer exemplary hospitality, worship, learning in community, service and mission, and generosity. The words *radical, passionate, intentional, risk-taking,* and *extravagant* only begin to describe the distinctive quality that characterizes their ministries.

Aspiring to excellence in service to God is deeply rooted in our faith heritage. God did not create the heavens and the earth and say, "It's good enough." Rather, Scripture describes God imbuing creation with superlatives: "God saw everything that he had made, and indeed, it was very good" (Genesis 1:31). Throughout Scripture, people offer their best and highest because God has given the best and highest.

Paul leads readers into his masterful and eloquent chapter on love with the words, "And I will show you a still more excellent way" (1 Corinthians 12:31). Love of God and neighbor surpasses all other strivings.

In Philippians, we find the admonition, "Whatever is true... honorable... just... pure... pleasing... commendable, if there is any excellence and if there is anything worthy of praise, think about these things" (Philippians 4:8). Christians should aspire to develop rich interior spiritual qualities and to reflect these in what they do.

Paul commends and encourages the Corinthian congregation for their excellence: "Now as you excel in everything—in faith, in speech, in knowledge, in utmost eagerness, and in our love for you—so we want you to also excel in this generous undertaking" (2 Corinthians 8:7).

In Paul's most direct appeal to excellence for the followers of Christ, he writes, "Since you are eager for spiritual gifts, strive to excel in them for building up the church" (1 Corinthians 14:12). Excellence serves the mission of strengthening the Body of Christ for ministry.

Biblical imperatives to *excel* do not match modern corporate uses of the word *excellence*. Spiritual motivation for excellence does not derive from market strategies, trying to outdo competitors to win customer affections, or striving to come out ahead while destructively climbing over weaker rivals to win at all costs. Excellence is not about superiority, outranking others, or seeking recognition.

Excellence in congregational ministry derives from the heartfelt commitment to offer our utmost for God's highest purposes. Excellence means to "live your life in a manner worthy of the gospel of Christ" (Philippians 1:27). It means, "striving side by side with one mind for the faith of the gospel" (Philippians 1:27). Pursuing excellence means cultivating the gifts of the Spirit in us and in others to the fullest to the glory of God. To value excellence in congregational ministry means that we take seriously John Wesley's expectation of a sanctifying grace with outward fruit and that we accept the lifelong task of seeking a still more excellent way in all that we do for Christ.

In their book, *Resurrecting Excellence: Shaping Faithful Christian Ministry* (Eerdmans, 2006), Greg Jones and Kevin Armstrong describe excellence in ministry as something perceptible and palpable. It's not only seen in "bodies, budgets, and buildings," but also in many other forms: the number of people whose lives are shaped by worship, hearts changed through Bible study, and a community life rich in Christ. Excellence may be revealed in the number of mission trips and outreach projects that transform lives and in the power and presence of God reflected in signs of forgiveness and gestures of reconciliation (p. 5).

In pursuing excellence, Jones and Armstrong ask, "Where is the presence and power of God being manifested in this congregation's life, in this person's life, in this person's pastoral leadership?" (p. 6). Do we see it in numerical growth, new programs, and outreach? In expanding stewardship or building new buildings? Do we see it in the pastor's hard work of reconciliation among factions in a community, in a congregation's willingness to care for those who are dying, or in a community's persistence in resisting injustice and fostering practices of mercy and justice? Excellence takes many forms.

The driving question for every pastor, church leader, and congregation is, "How do we cultivate gifts and talents in the very best way possible?"

In fulfilling the mission God entrusts to congregations, we cannot settle for what Jones and Armstrong have called "mediocrity masquerading as faithfulness" (p. 23). Vibrant, fruitful, growing congregations perform the five practices in exemplary ways because they keep repeating them, improving them, honing them, sharpening them, deepening them, and extending them. They never forget how important these practices are. Fruitful congregations do not ignore them, avoid them, or become too distracted with other things to do them well.

Aspiring to congregational excellence means pastors and church leaders look to the five practices and ask not only, "Are we performing these activities?" or "Are we doing these well?" but also, "Are we fulfilling these with excellence, in a manner worthy of the mission God has given us in Christ? Are we offering our best and highest?"

Is it fair to expect excellence from congregations, pastors, and church leaders? What does congregational excellence look like, and how do we cultivate it? What does clergy excellence look like, and how do we aspire to it? What does excellence in lay leadership look like, and how do we model it?

6.

When I was in the third grade, our family moved to Del Rio, a small town along the South Texas border with Mexico. Lutheran by heritage, we had attended the Methodist church in our previous community because it was conveniently located near where we lived. In Del Rio, my father worked on Sunday mornings, and my mother took care of my baby sister. So the first time we attended worship, my father, brother, and I went alone, stepping into a small evening prayer service at First Methodist Church. The gathering of mostly older adults sang hymns from the Cokesbury hymnal, and the pastor gave a brief message followed by a time for silent prayer during which everyone came forward and knelt at the communion rail. The service was simple, and the people were friendly. They seemed eager to meet us, and they invited us back.

A few days later, two church members knocked on our door, and my parents invited them into our small living room in the home we were renting. Dan Lloyd and Bill DeViney welcomed us to town and expressed their delight in our visiting the church. They met my mother, told her about the church nursery, and expressed the hope that she, too, would be able to come to church sometime soon.

As my father's schedule allowed, our family began to attend Sunday mornings, sitting in the balcony so that my parents would feel less self-conscious about their children. A new pastor was appointed to the church, and I can remember his opening sermon, in which he compared his first service to the preface of a book. I hold many powerful memories from my childhood and youth—the communion liturgy about our not being worthy so much as to gather up the crumbs under the table, the choir singing "Hallelujah" from Handel's *Messiah* on Easter, a revival in which the visiting Reverend Lin Henderson (who later became a bishop) called me by name from the pulpit and spoke to me of the beauty of the birth of Christ. I remember Mr. Palmer on the church organ, the duty given to me to collect the offering in the balcony, church suppers, slide shows about missions, and dramas and musicals that retold stories of the Bible. I was confirmed in sixth grade (after memorizing the Apostles' Creed, the Lord's Prayer, and the 23rd Psalm) and began to attend Sunday school and youth fellowship. I was invited to help with Vacation Bible School and became the AV (audiovisual) expert for church programs. I attended retreats, camps, back-packing trips, and service projects, all of them supported by youth directors and by numbers of volunteer sponsors. The youth chopped wood on a cold December morning to deliver mesquite to poor families with wood-burning stoves, made trips to nursing homes to sing for residents who spoke only Spanish, and helped at a center for mentally challenged adults. We trick-or-treated for UNICEF, washed cars to support the American Cancer Society, and took turns planning weekly youth programs on faith and contemporary issues. When I was about sixteen years old, the pastor, John Wesley Platt, preached a sermon on the call to ministry and afterwards handed me a brochure entitled, "Are You Called to Ministry?"

Through the years, my parents became more active, joining an adult Sunday school class, helping teach a children's class, volunteering on committees, helping with church dinners, and serving as ushers. Their best friends were people they came to know through the church; and over the years, they surrounded friends during times of grief, attended countless funerals, and celebrated the baptisms and weddings of their friends' children and grandchildren. Sometimes they visited people undergoing cancer treatments, and other times they were themselves the recipients of pastoral and collegial visits during times of illness and grief. My father served on the committee that planned the annual stewardship campaign, and even chaired it once. In their retired years, my mother and father took DISCIPLE Bible Study together, worked on weekly Meals on Wheels deliveries, and helped with the maintenance of the facility.

The ministry of First United Methodist Church in Del Rio that changed my life and the lives of my parents and family was simple and basic: initiating contact and welcoming strangers; providing engaging and authentic worship; offering opportunities for children, youth, and adults to grow in the knowledge and love of God; providing channels for meaningful service in the community; and helping members grow in giving. But by such ordinary congregational activities done consistently well, God shaped our lives in remarkable ways.

My parents were members of First United Methodist Church in Del Rio for more than thirty-five years, and with hindsight one can track their growing engagement and activity; the increased understanding of the faith; and the expanding sense of responsibility they felt for their church, community, and world. In thirty-five years they moved from having no meaningful church relationship and only nascent yearnings to learn more about faith to full involvement, leadership, and service in the church and to more profound and richer understandings of faith that have served them well. And the congregation's influence on my own life during the formative years between third grade and high school graduation has been immeasurable. Even if I had not responded to the call to ordained ministry, the rich experiences of community, faith, service, and generosity would have profoundly shaped my understanding the world, the ways of God, and the interior life.

If one could somehow take my parents' lives and extract from their experience all the influences accrued from thirty-five years of church membership, they would be entirely different people, unrecognizable from who they are now. If someone could remove all the shaping and learning and growing that came to them through friendships, worship services, Sunday school lessons, Bible studies, church suppers, private prayers, and mission projects, I cannot imagine who they would be, how they would see the world, in what ways they would relate to their community, or how they would experience the meaning and purpose of life and death. I have no idea how their knowledge and experience of peace, joy, hope, community, faith, and love would be different. They would be completely different people than who they have turned out to be.

The journey to faith that I've described in my family is repeated millions of times in tens of thousands of United Methodist churches. In congregations small, large, urban, suburban, and rural, and in wonderful and magnificently diverse ways, people are welcomed, hearts are changed, communities are formed, service is rendered, and people from all walks of life grow in grace and in the love of God and neighbor. Year in and year out, God uses congregations to make disciples, form faith, transform lives, and change the world.

Recently I attended the one hundredth anniversary celebration of a church that has a weekly attendance approaching three hundred people. At an evening banquet, church leaders honored those who had been members for thirty years or more, fifty years or more, and even seventy years or more. They recognized choir members who had faithfully sung for more than fifty years. Most memorable for me was the work of a church member who had meticulously prepared a church registry that included all the names of those who had been members during the entire one-hundred-year history of the church. The registry had more than 9,900 people listed. I found myself deeply moved thinking about nearly 10,000 people who through one congregation had felt themselves surrounded by the love of God, experienced enough of a sense of belonging to commit themselves to membership, opened their lives to God's transforming presence in weekly worship, and been nurtured in the faith as they matured in the love of God and neighbor. What a remarkable difference that congregation has made for the purposes of God in so many people's lives—in their families and among countless unnamed visitors, constituents, and non-members over the decades. What an incredible impact that congregation has had for the purposes of Christ on the community, on the state, and on the world. Imagine the life changing friendships gained, the sustaining grace discovered, the love given and received, the hope inspired, the joy found, the justice proclaimed, and the new life experienced in so many lives through this one single congregation.

Through ordinary practices done well over time, congregations make extraordinary differences in the lives of people. Through basic activities that express the prevenient, justifying, and sanctifying grace of God revealed in Christ, the church fulfills its mission. Making disciples involves a continuing cooperative effort on the part of the Holy Spirit and the church to bring people into relationship with God and neighbor through faith in Jesus Christ. The principal way God draws people into relationship with one another and with God is through congregations and faith communities. Churches are not clubs, social service agencies, networks of friends, or community centers. They are expressions of the Body of Christ, the means through which God reaches people with the gift and demand of God's grace.

God changes lives through congregations, and this places upon pastors and congregational leaders the awesome and joyful responsibility of cultivating strength, health, clarity of purpose, and faithfulness in practice in congregational life so that the mission of Christ thrives. The exemplary and repeated practices of Radical Hospitality, Passionate Worship, Intentional Faith Development, Risk-Taking Mission and Service, and Extravagant Generosity are the time-tested, theologically sound, and effective means congregations use to fulfill their mission with excellence and fruitfulness to the glory of God. These practices stir the church to unexpected renewal and expanded vision, just as they have for centuries. Congregations are called to change the world, not just keep their doors open. God works through congregations to transforms lives.

Conversation Questions:

- How would your church look if your congregation committed to performing these five practices with excellence? What would change? Who would be with you who is not currently in your congregation? What excites you about that? What scares you about that?
- How would personally practicing these five practices with greater intentionality shape your own faith journey? How would they change your habits, values, and attitudes? How would practicing then change your relationship to God, to the church, and to your neighbor?